Beyond the Downbeat

Choral Rehearsal Skills and Techniques

Sandra Willetts

Abingdon Press
Nashville

Beyond the Downbeat
Choral Rehearsal Skills and Techniques

This book is printed on acid-free, recycled paper.

ISBN 0-687-07484-3

04 05 06 07 08 09 — 10 9 8 7 6 5 4 3

*To all the good folks who,
at some point
during the past twenty-five years,
have attended my workshops,
but most especially
to the two of you
who were well-behaved.*

Special thanks to Dr. Barbara Caughran and to
Dr. Susan Fleming for their invaluable assistance.

Contents

Introduction

A conductor with a clear physical gesture has the potential to be an effective music maker. But a conductor who has mastered the music to be made, who recognizes the needs of the group to make the music, and who knows how to rehearse that music has a better opportunity to realize the fullest potential in the art of music making.

The following chapters are all necessary areas of study for the conductor who envisions himself or herself as having this potential and who has the motivation and the self-discipline to meet the challenge.

Chapter One

Vocal/Choral Warm-ups

If we consider that the conductor is the only active musician who does not actually produce a sound, it should heighten our resolve to learn about the instrument that does! The choral conductor's instrument is the human voice—someone else's voice. In other words, our instrument is the choir. As conductors, we have to rely on the collective voices of our choir to function as our instrument; and the care of this instrument is paramount to a successful performance of the music, not to mention the well-being of each voice and the person who owns it. Whatever your goals as the conductor, the improvement and protection of your instrument should be primary.

If you as the conductor are a trained singer, you already know that the act of singing is definitely a physical activity, sometimes thought of as an athletic event. If you are an instrumentalist, particularly a keyboardist, you may not have conceptualized singing in so dramatic a manner. Believe it! Simply put, the tone that is produced is a pitch on the breath. Tone is breath passing through the vocal folds or the vocal cords, vibrating at a specific pitch and resonating in the throat, mouth, and nasal cavities. Breath is tone supporting. Breath is life supporting! Good breathing requires good muscle tone and aerobic conditioning. Both breath control and breath capacity can be enhanced with good physical conditioning.

When we recognize the physical commitment involved in singing, we can compare the needs of the singer and the athlete. Both must train for peak capacity and endurance—training that can result in peak performances. Unfortunately, you as the conductor have absolutely no control over your choir's physical conditioning. You can only cajole them (repeatedly) into taking good care of themselves. What you can control is a routine of preparing the singer to sing. Just like the athlete, a singer needs to warm up the necessary muscles before expecting them to work effectively. The time you devote to awakening the body, the breath, and the voice will be time well spent. The singers will be more alert, energized, and focused; and together you can accomplish short-term goals more quickly and efficiently. You are also working toward the ever-present long-term goal of a better singing quality. You will be consistently reinforcing good vocal habits. A good vocal warm-up session should be like a good voice lesson!

Here are some of my favorite warm-up exercises.

Physical Exercises

First, start with a few simple stretches. These can be done with few verbal instructions. You execute and they copy. A quiet atmosphere will help them begin to concentrate.

1. Arms reach in front. Clasp hands and rotate, palms pushing outward. Hold the push for eight seconds, then relax. (*Stretches back muscles.*)
2. Arms reach overhead. Clasp hands and rotate, palms pushing up. Hold for eight seconds, then relax. (*Stretches side muscles.*)
3. Tilt right ear to right shoulder. Hold for four seconds, then relax. (*Stretches left neck muscles.*)
4. Reverse to left side and repeat. (*Stretches right neck muscles.*)
5. Drop chins, excuse me, chin, gently to the chest and roll slowly to the right and back to the center. Repeat to the left. (*Stretches and relaxes neck muscles.*)
6. Shake out shoulders, arms, and hands and go right into the first breathing exercise with as few words as possible.

Breathing Exercises

1. Place hands on sides at the waist and sip steadily as though through a straw for four seconds. Expansion should be felt at the sides while the upper chest remains quiet. Exhale, blowing out steadily for four seconds. You count out loud. Repeat once.

(Encourage the singers to fill to the bottom of the lungs and, when exhaling, to *gently* push out and down so as not to let the muscles around the lungs collapse.)

2. Sip through the straw again but exhale with four short pulses, followed by one long pulse. Follow the rhythmic pattern shown in the Breathing Exercise that follows. Use a hissing sound like the first sound in the word *center.* Repeat three times, using the quarter rest at the end of the second bar to get a good catch breath for each of the two remaining sequences. Conduct this exercise. It will be good practice for you to execute good preparatory beats and cutoffs. The second chapter of my book *Upbeat Downbeat* covers this more thoroughly.

Breathing Exercise

Vocal Exercises

1. Using the same rhythmic pattern found in the second breathing exercise, replace the hissing sound with the word *mum* and sing it on a comfortable pitch. Close to the second *m* immediately, even on the long note. I like to use *mum* because, by closing immediately to that second *m*, the whole word becomes mostly a hum. In a hum, the sound can come only through the nose. This means that it has automatically traveled up to the dome or mask, through the nasal passages and eventually escapes from the nose. The trick is to get the singers to route everything that high. Obviously, when the mouth is open, sound will escape from this larger opening first. A combination of using all the resonating chambers with the sound

escaping from both the nose and the mouth is optimal. Remind your singers of this often and return to singing on *mum* frequently. They must memorize what it feels like to sing in the dome or mask, and humming is nature's way of achieving that automatically.

Vocal Exercise 1

mum   mum   mum   mum   mum

Repeat this exercise beginning a half step higher. Be careful not to extend out of a comfortable range. Reverse the direction and extend below the original pitch, then return to it. Another variation would be to sing it in a *legato* articulation, rather than the *staccato* articulation that is indicated in the exercise. Also vary the tempo, and always conduct.

2. Using the same rhythmic pattern, substitute the syllables *mee—meh—mah—moh—moo*. Start on a medium pitch, move up and/or down in half steps, vary the articulation and tempo, and continue to conduct. (For a discussion of pure vowels and the importance of diction, see chapter 2 of this book.)

Vocal Exercise 2

mee   meh   mah   moh   moo

3. Using a sequence of any two vowels, sing them to the rhythmic pattern as shown in Vocal Exercise 3 in a

legato style. Begin with a minor third, expand up to a perfect fifth, then reverse the direction, eventually returning to the minor third. I like to start with *ah-oo*. If you can get them to sing *oo* out of an *ah* "space in their face," you may qualify for sainthood! You can also start with the more focused sound, *oo-ah*. Just be sure they are singing the first *oo* with the resonance and purity that you will eventually expect. Other variations include using different vowel sequences and beginning on different pitches.

Vocal Exercise 3

ah oo ah oo ah   ah oo ah oo ah

4. This exercise provides an opportunity for improving articulation and agility. It is energizing and can be fun. Do it as detached as possible and do as many repetitions as you like, each beginning a half step higher or lower. For variation, sing it *legato* but insist that the changes in syllables remain clear.

Vocal Exercise 4

mee meh mah moh   mee meh mah moh   mee meh mah moh moo (etc.)

5. Add an octave plus one note to the third sequence of the previous exercise, and it becomes even more fun. And for almost more fun than you can tolerate, continue adding sequences to the beginning of the exercise and move the octave run to the fourth, fifth, and even sixth sequence. All of this, of course, is to be

Vocal Exercise 5

mee meh mah moh mee meh mah moh

mee meh mah moh mee meh mah moh moo

done on one breath. Remember to conduct. See if you can help them identify when to move to the octave with your conducting gesture and not by shouting a verbal direction at them.

6. Another octave plus one exercise provides a good warm-up opportunity when you are totally pressed for time. I call it my "get off the bus and sing" exercise. In reality, it is called a "lip trill," though a "lip buzz" would be a better description. Buzz the lips on random pitches just to get the buzz started, perhaps in a siren effect. When most of them have the buzz going, establish a unison pitch. Sing, while buzzing, an octave plus one, up and down the scale. If your lips stall out, it means you probably did not get a good breath. That's why this exercise is such a good one. It is the combination of enough breath and the agility of the lip muscles that together create the buzz. Repeat, beginning a half step up or down as often as time allows, or when their lips give out—whichever happens first. Some people physically cannot do a lip buzz. Allow those singers to do the exercise on "la" or other combinations of consonants and vowels.

Vocal Exercise 6

Lip Trill or Lip Buzz

7. A great exercise for tuning is to begin on a unison or an octave pitch and move in half steps—one section moving up and one section moving down. (Define your sections by gender at first and then get more creative by having the sopranos and tenors team up against the altos and basses. If space permits, let them stand together in a circle and really hone in on a unison pitch.) Continue this outward motion until the interval of a minor sixth is achieved; then reverse the direction, moving at half step intervals and returning to the original unison or octave pitch. To arrive at the starting pitch without anyone having to adjust is the goal. Don't be discouraged if it does not work right away. Keep at it and they will rise to the challenge eventually. It will become their goal as well as yours. Yet another reason for sainthood!

Vocal Exercise 7

8. The final exercise is not only good for warming up the voice and the ears, but also provides a great teaching aid for learning to sing intervals. Use *mum* or your favorite syllable, or sing the letter names of the pitches. This will enhance their concentration and their awareness of the spelling of the actual interval. Two for one! Actually three! Continue the

Vocal Exercise 8

15

outward motion until you have reached an octave. At this point, you will be encompassing two octaves so be sure to start with a pitch that you can sing both an octave above and an octave below. I often sing this exercise myself, sometimes in the car, sometimes in the fairway. It helps keep my voice and my ears up to par.

Some Final Thoughts on Warm-Ups

Do all of these exercises in a comfortable volume, perhaps at *mezzo forte* (*mf*). If the singing is too soft, the muscles won't be adequately involved. If the singing is too loud, the muscles will be overinvolved. Stay with the happy medium in both volume and pitch, at least in the beginning of your warm-up.

Do your best not to lapse into a predictable routine by using the same exercises each rehearsal. The singers will pay less attention and just go mindlessly through the motions. Remember, part of your job is to keep them confused—uh—I mean keep them focused on the task, always functioning at a high level of performance, even while doing vocal exercises.

Obviously, you will not do each of these exercises and their many variations at each rehearsal. Your choices should reflect the needs of the music scheduled for that particular rehearsal. If you have conducted a successful warm-up, the singers will be focused and ready to go. Capitalize on that eagerness and finish with an exercise that will lead you right into the first piece. For instance, if you begin with a "chirpy," Handelian chorus, vocal exercises 4 or 5 would be appropriate. If your opener is something soft and sustained, vocal exercise 2 (in a slow tempo, with a *legato* articulation) would suffice. If you can manage to end in the key of the opening piece—very impressive! In order to avoid breaking their concentration, have the first piece of the evening already at hand. Of course, you have put the entire rehearsal order on the board before they arrive, haven't you?

If you are absolutely down to crunch time and there are still notes to be learned, ignore all of the above and create your own exercises around the troubling passages. Sing them in unison, on *mum*, at a slow tempo to be sped up when appropriate, or whatever the situation demands. If you simply do not have time to warm up at all, be sure that the first piece is not the fastest and loudest of the rehearsal. At the very least, let them warm up on that first piece. You would be wise not to be terribly critical until they have sung awhile. Give them a chance to find a groove.

Announce to your choir that the warm-up will start ten minutes before the scheduled rehearsal time. If they cannot attend, you'll expect them to arrive already warmed up and therefore join "a work in progress." Do not try this until after you have them addicted to the concept of warming up, and they have experienced the value of it first hand!

I realize that all of this seems very idealistic. It *is* idealistic! Don't we strive for the ideal? If we are trying to "make a joyful noise to the Lord," then it should be the very best. Now see, I'm getting excited and out comes the soapbox! Whatever your current conducting expertise, *you* are the leader. If you have accepted the responsibility as the choir leader, then one of your responsibilities is to garner as much expertise as you can. It will not happen overnight, and it will take concentrated and consistent application. If you have had formal training in music, there are still things you can learn. None of us knows everything, although admittedly some of us may act as if we do. If there is one thing I have learned in thirty-plus years of teaching and conducting, it is that it takes a lifetime to master both. I can be a better teacher and a better conductor tomorrow than I am today, and so can you.

Chapter Two

Diction

Diction can be defined as "the degree of clarity and distinctness of pronunciation in speech and singing."[2] Singers should strive to sing text clearly and distinctly. As choral conductors, we train our choirs to do that very thing. After all, words separate vocalists from all other instruments. The words give us distinction. If we treat them with the utmost importance, we will be rewarded many times over. Clarity is our first reward; the words will be understood and the message will be heard. But think about all the possible by-products of good diction. In addition to clarity, your choir will have (1) a better singing quality; (2) a better ensemble sound; (3) better intonation; (4) better articulation; (5) and more expressive music. Have I got your attention?

First, better diction will produce a better singing quality. Since we sing on the vowels, we will certainly sound better if we all sing the vowels properly. The teaching of singing is done through the vowels. There is no other way to do it. Robert Shaw used to say, "The vowels give our singing beauty; the consonants give it drama."

Second, singing the consonants together will improve the rhythmic unity (ensemble) of the choir, not only at the beginning of phrases but also at problematic breathing places and at the ends of phrases. Also, we must attack and release both the consonants and vowels at the same time. And, as we deal with the vanishing vowel of the dreaded diphthong, we must "vanish" at the same time. Our ensemble will be better.

Third, if the vowels are not unified throughout the choir, the intonation will suffer. Assuming that everyone has the same vowel, particularly at the ends of phrases and usually at the final chord, everyone has to sing that vowel exactly alike. The sound must be unified and, in order for the chord to snap into tune, it also must happen at the same time. For instance, in the word *amen,* everyone must arrive at the *eh* vowel together. If the sopranos are luxuriating through a mellifluous *m,* the intonation and the ensemble will be ragged. Sing unified vowels on the beat and sing intense, rhythmic consonants so that both intonation and ensemble will have a fighting chance. If the music negates the possibility of the entire choir singing the words at the same time (polyphonic as opposed to homophonic), then work to unify the vowels and consonants within each section.

Fourth, in dealing with articulation, if your choir needs to improve the *legato* line, work to intensify the vocal consonants. Most of the consonants with pitch are sung with a closed, or partially closed, mouth (*m, n,* and *ng*) or lips and/or tongue that are focused into a small pressurized opening (*r, v, th,* and *z*). Though the mouth is open when shaping *l,* the high tongue does change the shape of the opening. Since the vowels are sung with an open mouth, a sound that is sent through a smaller opening needs to be a bit louder (more intense) to balance the sounds from a larger opening. Intensify the vocal consonants to match the volume of the vowels around them, maintaining a constant breath pressure. This will greatly improve the singing *legato* line of your choir.

If your choir needs to improve the opposite articulation, the detached or *staccato* style in singing, work to intensify and "rhythmicize" the explosive and sibilant consonants. These consonants will provide you with great material for this style of articulation. The term "rhythmicize" means to shorten the actual rhythm of the note to provide time for the execution of the consonant (if there is one), and to get a breath for the next phrase. This is helpful when the composer has not allowed for a breath within the notation of the music. Most of these places are obvious. For instance, although almost none of the hymns we sing have quarter or half rests at the ends of each phrase, we automatically breathe because of the punctuation marks in the text and because by then we probably need it! In music that is not so familiar, especially in polyphonic music, it is more difficult to make those decisions. But make them we must. The members of the choir will breathe when they find it necessary anyway. For the sake of ensemble, you as the conductor must make those decisions and do it before the first rehearsal.

Fifth, if you incorporate these suggestions on diction into your rehearsals, your choir will sing with more power, more drama, and more expression. You should also monitor the strong and weak syllables of the text, the natural word inflections. It is amazing to me how choirs, when asked, can speak the text with the proper inflections after they have just sung the same words without any inflection at all. They need constant (and pleasant) encouragement to think for themselves and not to leave every decision up to us. For example, the words *father* and *mother,* when sung will sound like "fah-thuh" and "muh-thuh." Ask the choir to speak those words with a more natural inflection and you will hear "FAH-thuh" and "MUH-thuh." Wouldn't it be nice if we could skip that step and just expect our choirs to make the easy choices themselves?

Finally, don't wait until the last minute to discuss the meaning and the message of the text. We know that our choirs are more committed and more communicative in their music making if they understand the text and can somehow identify with it. The sooner everyone is "on the same page," the sooner everyone can enjoy the process. Choral music is all about enjoying the process. If we lived only for that perfect performance, we would never be fulfilled. Our profession is definitely "in the process."

Diction Chart

Now that I've convinced you of the benefits of dealing in depth with diction (say that three times quickly), let's get to the specifics. The following chart of vowels and consonants has undergone many revisions. Dr. Clarence (Clancy) Martin gave it to me while I was an undergraduate student at Westminster College in New Wilmington, Pennsylvania in the early 1960s. Most of my voice teachers and colleagues since then have added their opinions along the way. You may copy the chart for each of your choir members or enlarge to poster size and hang it in your choir room. It is important to keep the concept of dealing carefully with vowels and consonants constantly in front of them.

VOWELS AND CONSONANTS
The Singer's Scale of Pure American English Vowel Sounds

Tongue Vowels   (Neutral)   Lip Vowels

		*				*					*		
[i]	[e]	[ɪ]	[ɛ]	[æ]	[a]	[ɑ]	[ʌ]	[ɔ]	[ɜ]	[o]	[ʊ]	[u]
Nee	nay	nit	net	nat	nigh	nah	nut	naught	nerd	no	nook	noo

Closed ———— Open ———— Closed

The schwa is an unstressed vowel sound as in the *a* of *about.* [ə]

DIPHTHONGS

A	=	ay – ih, as in *day*	[e ɪ]
I	=	ah – ih, as in *night*	[ɑ ɪ]
O	=	oh – oo, as in *no*	[o u]
U	=	ee – oo, as in *you*	[i u]
OW	=	ah – oo, as in *now*	[ɑ u]
OY	=	augh – ih, as in *boy*	[ɔ ɪ]

CONSONANTS

Vocal			Sub-Vocal		
L	–	love	B	–	body
M	–	mother	D	–	do
N	–	no	G	–	go
NG	–	ing	J	–	jump
R	–	ring			
V	–	very			
W	–	word			
TH	–	this			
Z	–	zebra			

* Use only the primary (or first) vowel sound of this word.

Explosives		**Sibilants**			**Aspirates**		
C	– cart	C	–	center	WH	–	when
K	– kick	CH	–	church	H**	–	heart
P	– pop	F	–	father			
Q	– quick	S	–	sister			
T	– tot	SH	–	show			
		TH	–	thought			
		X	–	extra			

** H can also be silent, as in the word *hour.*

The first terms you see on the chart are **"Tongue Vowels"** and **"Lip Vowels."** This is a simple, but important concept. If we agree that *ah* is the neutral vowel sound, it can function as our point of reference. Every sound to the left of *ah* (*ee* up to *ah*) is shaped by the tongue. The higher the tongue, the brighter or more closed the vowel. The trick for the *ee* sound is to get the singers to keep their lips quiet while the tongue shapes the vowel. Most amateurs are used to grinning from ear to ear when singing a bright *ee* sound. That can tense the lip and neck muscles and certainly cramps the resonating space.

Every sound to the right of *ah* (*oo* back to *ah*) is shaped by the lips. The more puckered the lips, the darker or more closed the vowel. The trick here is to pull the lips around the *ah* opening without disturbing the space. Most amateur singers will shut down on the inside to sing the *oo* sound, causing it to sound pinched and cramped.

Our major goal is to find the optimum opening for the *ah* vowel and sing the other vowel sounds through that same opening, adjusting the tongue or the lips respectively. The "space in your face" remains constant while the tongue and lips change! Of course, there will be adjustments for consonants and very high or low pitches, but if you can convince amateur singers to think about tongue and lip vowels, it will improve their sound immediately. To find the optimum *ah*, ask them to "bite an apple." The image of that usually gets them to open comfortably wide, showing a bit of the top front teeth. Not everyone will have the same amount of opening so don't expect them to all look alike. Some have bigger mouths than others. This we know already.

Next on the chart, find the **IPA (International Phonetic Alphabet)** symbols. Under each is found a word whose vowel sound matches the sound of that symbol. The IPA is a great tool, especially if you do a lot of singing in foreign languages. The symbols are the same for every language, hence their description as "international." They function as a type of shorthand and can be very useful when written right into a score. For example, in singing the word *desire,* you may want to put the symbol [I] above the first syllable. It will be a visual reminder that you want them to sing "d(*ih*) - zire" and not "d(*ee*) - sire." Having the symbol written there will also give you a better chance of hearing the mistake if it happens. It means that you have thought about it ahead of time and will be ready with an easy fix if they should falter. Remember, if some are singing [I] and some are singing [i], the chord will not tune! This will only be helpful to you if you recognize the symbols as well as you do *ih* and *ee.* The "Closed — Open — Closed" illustration should be self-explanatory and reinforces what was said above about creating the most open sound, which is *ah.*

The **schwa** is a very useful sound, especially when pitches extend far enough above the staff to render pure vowels acoustically impossible. Every vowel, given a high enough pitch, modifies to a schwa. Technically, this is called Vowel Modification. Starting on a medium pitch, sing a pure *ee* [i] and see how high you can sing while maintaining the pure sound. You will not get far above the staff before it wants to open. Sing high enough and it will open all the way to a schwa [ə]. Sometimes you will see this sound described as *uh,* but try to get used to the upside-down, backward *e* [ə] instead. Remember, the schwa is an unaccented, or unstressed sound.

Now everyone's favorite—the **diphthong**! First, learn how to pronounce the word. It's not "*dip*-thong" with an explosive *p* in the middle. It is "*difff*-thong." I apologize for harping, but if we are going to correct someone's pronunciation using a technical term, we should pronounce it correctly. A retired English professor in your choir will call a foul on you, and you know how they love to correct your mistakes! The **diphthong** often creates problems for choirs. It is a Greek word that literally means "two sounds." The choir must be able to sing the exact sounds you want and move to the second sound simultaneously. This second sound is sometimes called the "vanishing vowel." The primary or first vowel sound is the one that needs to be sustained. The second one needs to be voiced as one leaves the note, hence the "vanishing" concept. Many amateur singers will go immediately to the second sound, producing a pop style; others do not voice the second vowel enough for the word to be understood. One sounds like "ol' blue eyes" singing "naheeet an' deheee"; the other sounds *terribly* British: "naaaht and deh." Somewhere in the middle would be good.

The five categories of **consonants** conclude our diction chart. Other books will have alternate choices for the same concepts, but these are my favorites because they come closest to actually describing the sound production needed for their respective categories.

- The **Vocal Consonants** are voiced. They can be sung on a pitch.
- The **Sub-Vocal Consonants** feel as though they are produced under the larynx, or under the voice. They cannot be sung on a pitch. Only the vowel sounds that follow these "ferocious four" have pitch.
- The **Explosives** need an explosion of air to create the sounds.
- The **Sibilants** are sung on an air stream.
- The **Aspirates** category may be the most difficult one. The *WH* words (*what, when, why, where, and which*) should be started with a puff of air. Blow through the *WH*. They do not begin with an *oo* vowel sound. The *oo* follows the puff of air. Because our speech has become so casual, we don't often hear these words spoken properly either. Start them with the puff of air, and clarity and drama will be your immediate rewards.
- The *H* in *heart* is also aspirated, but the problem is much greater. The vowel that immediately follows the air is the most open vowel, *ah*. Because the mouth is so open, it is

difficult, if not impossible, to focus the puff of air. It takes so much breath to start this word that only the most conscientious singer will even think about it. Try to sing the first phrase of the hymn, "Holy, Holy, Holy." If you have aspirated the first two *H*'s properly, you will probably need a breath before the third one. In fact, to get the most out of these words, a breath before each would help.

• The **silent** *H*, as in *hour*, is indeed silent.

Here are a few additional tips about certain consonants beginning with *R*. This rascal can be produced at least three ways: it can be voiced, flipped, or rolled. The American tradition is to voice or sing it.

Always sing an *R* when it
• begins a word (as in *river*)
• if it is in between two vowels (as in *arise*)

Never sing an *R* when it
• ends the word (as in *river*)
• if it comes before another consonant (as in *earth*)
• if it comes before a silent vowel (as in *here*)

You may flip the R
• in words that have a double *R* (as in *sorrow*)
• when singing words on high notes that are more easily produced with a flipped rather than with a voiced *R*
• when opting for more drama in certain words (such as *grief*)
• in operatic music
• if you are singing in a foreign language that requires it
• (If you cannot flip an R, just substitute a D.)

When to roll the R
• *Never*, except for extreme dramatic effect

Notice that the combination *TH* appears in two categories. This is not a mistake. One is voiced, the other is a sibilant. When dealing with the word *with*, it can be your choice as to which *TH* sound to use. When it is possible, use the voiced sound to create a better *legato* line.

The most problematic sound of all is the *SSSSS!* In order to ensure a unified beginning when a phrase starts with *S,* ask the choir to start the *S* on the beat, not before it. I know we agreed that the vowel is sung on the beat, but in the case of the hissing *S* (also the buzzing consonants *V* and *Z*) you will get an uneven hissing or buzzing sound unless you convince the choir to try this. The vowel will still be on the beat, but the *S* will be so close to it that the hiss factor should be eliminated.

There are people in my choirs who have chosen never to sing a final *S* ever again—for fear of loss of life or limb. Do I sound amused? They have learned that it can cause me to go ballistic! Actually, I only go ballistic over having to repeat the same instruction forty-seven times! I admit that I am somewhat obsessed with getting final *S*'s together. But in self-defense, that prolonged hissing sound is not music. It is just hissing! Making beautiful music requires a type of sculpting away anything that is ugly so that only the beauty is visible—or in our case, audible. Here is the fix! When just asking them to sing the final *S* on a particular beat as in rhythmicize, does not work, ask them to substitute the letter *T* for the *S*. We'll use the word *dos,* which becomes "dot." Ask them to speak it and be aware of the time that is taken to execute that *T.* Return to the original word *dos,* and ask them to take no more time in the execution of the *S* than it took for the *T.* Repeat this process until they get it or until the rehearsal is over—whichever happens first. A word of caution: If you are successful in fixing it for the moment, this book does not come with a guarantee that it will stay fixed!

To Link or Not to Link

In an effort to sing a more *legato* line, many singers will link words together that, for the listener, actually changes the meaning of the text. There are many examples, some humorous, some sad, and some unprintable. Here are just a few. No doubt you can add your own.

- "Gladly the cross I'd bear" (gladly the cross-eyed bear)
- "Lead on, O King Eternal" (lee don O kinky turtle)

- "Weep oh mine eyes and cease not" (wee poh my nighs and see snot)
- "Let us pray" and "Let us in" (leh tuh spray and leh tuh sin)
- "Beautiful eyes" (beautiful lies)
- "And He walks with me and He talks with me" (Andy walks with me, Andy talks with me)

And my personal favorite, "Mairzy Doats," an old 1943 tune with words and music by Drake, Hoffman, and Livingston.

> Mairzy doats and dozy doats
> and liddle lamzy divey,
> a kiddley divey too,
> wouldn't you? [3]

My computer just blew a gasket in spell check. My daddy sang this tune to me when I was a little girl. The problem was that he must have known only this much of it. Until recently at one of my workshops, when someone offered this as another example of linking nightmares, I had never seen or heard the bridge of the chorus with the real words. I thought it was all nonsense syllables. For the few others who may be still in the dark, here are those words.

> Mares eat oats and does eat oats
> And little lambs eat ivy.
> A kid will eat ivy too,
> Wouldn't you? [4]

It still makes no sense, but it is a great example of when to link and when not to! My rule is simple: *When one can link to enhance the line without clouding the text, do so.* Always link to enhance the *legato* line. Never link if new words will be formed as a result.

So how can we ever sing a *legato* line again? I have found the term "paper space" to be very useful. Ask the choir to separate only the tiny space of a piece of paper before the next word, if it creates a new word. They should not create enough space for a breath, just enough to avoid creating the new word if the previous consonant is slapped into it. When the next word starts with a vowel, some folks will object and call this a glottal attack. Nay! Nay! With a glottal attack there is a definite holding back of the breath. The paper space is just a suspension of airflow without actually holding the air back. A glottal sound produces a bump in the line while the paper space just aerates it.

What about double consonants? "Put down" is a good example. You have at least three choices as to how to sing these words:

1. Explode the *T* and also intensify the *D*. This will produce two separate sounds and be perfectly understood.
2. Explode the *T*, add an *uh* sound to separate the two consonants, and intensify the *D*. If overdone, this could begin to sound like "*uh* Lawrence *uh* Welk *uh.*"
3. Implode the *T* and go right to the intensified *D*, creating only one sound but still being understood.

The choice is yours, imagine that! And that brings me to another of my favorite sayings: ***Casual diction for casual music—classical diction for classical music.***

Pop, folk, and country music can be described as casual music. We know what classical music means. This is not to say that casual music is not as good as classical music. It is just a different category and should not be subjected to the same formal rules of pronunciation. Regarding vowels, it is the old argument of *either* ("*ah-ee*-thuh" or "*ee*-thuh") and *tomato* ("tuh-*may*-toh" or "tuh-*mah*-to"). Both are correct if used in the correct setting. Another example is the word *little*. If it comes up in a pop/folk song or dialect, you would relax the consonants and probably sing "liddle," electing not to sing an explosive *T*. If it is an art song or classical music, you would probably sing "little," with the *T* exploded. Actually, this is your choice. There really are no hard and fast rules, just good musical taste. Use your best judgment and your best ears and hear what really comes across to the listeners. The fact that you have thought about it and have made all the choices before the first rehearsal is the important thing. Didn't I say that already?

Miscellaneous Concerns

- Sometimes we are used to singing words differently from how we say them. The word *evil* is the most common example. We say "ee-*vul*," but we feel the need to sing "ee-*vihl*." It just sounds too strange to sing it the first way. But look it up in the dictionary and you'll find that that is the way it is supposed to be pronounced. If the note value is relatively short for the second syllable, I would sing "ee-*vul.*" If the second syllable has to be sustained for any significant length of time, I would brighten the vowel to *ih.* It just sounds too ugly to sing a schwa for very long.

- A lot of words begin with "be" or "de" as in *beside* and *deliver.* If you are not sure of the correct pronunciation, look it up in the dictionary. It should be "*bih*-side" and "*dih*-liver." If you sing "*dee*-liver," you are talking about major surgery!

- One more rule: *DANIEL SITTETH!* I will quote this strange rule from the Queen of English Diction herself, Madeleine Marshall, from her book, *The Singer's Manual of English Diction.* [5] Every singer and every conductor should own a copy. "Syllables spelled with *u* or *ew* are pronounced *yu* after the consonants that appear in *DANIEL SITTETH.* The words in question are those in which a syllable spelled with either *u* or *ew* follows any one of these consonants: *d, n, l, s, t,* or *th.* Here is a simple device for remembering these consonants: They are the consonants in the two words *DANIEL SITTETH.* We are not concerned with the identity of Daniel or the fact that he sits in the formal present tense. The simple declarative sentence, *DANIEL SITTETH,* is merely a useful memory aid." This affects words like *duty, new, elude, suit, tune,* and *enthuse.* They are all pronounced with the *yu* sound. There are exceptions to this rule, but you are going to have to read her book to get them. Consider this much just a teaser.

- Another valuable diction book is simply called *Diction,* by John Moriarty.[6] It is very complete, very specific and will provide a great resource for other languages as well.

Finally, do you solemnly swear to approach diction with the enthusiasm of a zealot, the persistence of a bulldog, and the patience of Job? Your choir won't know what hit them, or rather, what hit you! Don't be disheartened if they don't jump on board as fast as you want them to. It is a slow but steady process. **Just stay with it and you will, in fact, reap the rewards of better singing, better ensemble, better intonation, better articulation and better expressivity.** In other words, you will have a better choir and will make better music. Everyone wins, including those listening.

Chapter Three
Singing in Latin

Do not skip this chapter! Once you realize that English requires of your choir *thirteen* different vowel sounds (you did count them, didn't you?), while Latin requires only *five* (have I got a deal for you!), you will become an advocate for singing in Latin! Having read chapter 2, you will remember that in order to tune a chord, the vowel sound must be unified. Would you rather unify thirteen vowels or five vowels? **Your choir will have a better chance of singing in tune when they sing in Latin.**

"But," you say, "my congregation/audience won't be able to understand the words!" A simple way to ensure that the congregation understands what the choir is singing is to print the text (with translation when necessary) in the bulletin or program. Works every time. What people see, they are more likely to hear and understand.

"But," you say, "my congregation/audience does not like music in Latin." Have you actually conducted a poll? Have they heard enough Latin to even have an opinion? It has been my experience that congregations/audiences like what they are used to—what is familiar to them. Have you given them the opportunity to become familiar with the beautiful sound of the pure vowels in Latin? Don't sell them or your choir short. Singing a beautiful piece of music with a meaningful text in its original language, especially Latin, can enhance the aesthetic experience greatly.

Singing a translation from Latin presents other problems. If the translation attempts to be true to the original, the accents of the text may not line up with the accents of the music. If it is a free translation, there may be only a hint of the original message that gets through.

You can avoid all these problems by singing the piece in Latin. And just think, by the time your choir has sung five or six pieces in Latin, they will be five or six times better at singing pure vowels! You will be able to reinforce the concept of the pure vowel as you teach them the text and the music. Two for one!

Okay, so you have to learn a few rules concerning the consonants. Here's the "deal" of which I spoke. The following is a short summary of the basic rules of Latin pronunciation. My sources are three wonderful books, all of which should be in your own library: *The Correct Pronunciation of Latin According to Roman Usage; Diction: Italian, Latin, French, German* (mentioned in chapter 2); and *Translations and Annotations of Choral Repertoire, Volume I: Sacred Latin Texts.*[7]

Be sure to practice the pronunciation before you demonstrate for your choir. It will not build their confidence if they hear you stumbling over it.

A Summary of Latin Pronunciation Rules

Vowels

A	=	*ah* as in *father*
E	=	*eh* as in *net*
I (Y)	=	*ee* as in *see*
O	=	*aw* as in *yawn*
U	=	*oo* as in *moo*

Diphthongs

AE or OE	=	*eh* (the same sound)
AI	=	*ah-ee* (two distinct sounds)
OU	=	*aw-oo* (two distinct sounds)
EI	=	*eh-ee* (two distinct sounds)
AU	=	*ah-oo* (two distinct sounds)

When *ui, ue, ua,* and *uo* are preceded by *q* or *ng*, go quickly to the second vowel.

Qui	=	*koo-EE*

Consecutive vowels require two separate sounds.

Filii	=	*fee-lee-ee*

Consonants
First the easy ones:

B, F, K, M, N, P, Q, V	All pronounced as in English.
D, L, T	Dental as in Italian (the tongue is forward and touches the back of the top front teeth).
R	Flipped as in Italian.
J	Is a glide as in *you* (Jesu = *Yeh-soo*).
PH	Always treated as an *f* as in *phantom*. (Seraphim = *Seh-rah-feem*)
TH	Always treated as a *t* (which is dental). (Catholicam = *Kah-taw-lee-kahm*)
Z	Sounds like *dz* as in *lads*. (Lazarus = *Lah-dzah-roos*)

And the less easy ones (only because there are choices):

C	Soft *ch* as in *church* when it precedes *e, i, ae, oe*. (Fecit = *Feh-cheet*; Coelum = *Cheh-loom*)
C	Hard *k* as in *cart* when it precedes consonants and the vowels *a, o, u*. (Credo = *Creh-daw*; Saecula = *Seh-koo-lah*)
CC	Sounds like *tch* as in *latch* when it precedes *e, i, ae, oe*. (Ecce = *Eh-tcheh*)
CH	Always a hard *k* as in *cart*. (Christe = *Kree-steh*)

G	Soft *j* as in *gemini* when it precedes *e, i, ae, oe*. (Unigenite = *Oo-nee-jeh-nee-teh*)
G	Hard *g* as in *go* when it precedes consonants and the vowels *a, o, u*. (Gloria = *Glaw-ree-ah*; Ergo = *Ehr-gaw*)
GN	Sounds like *ny* as in *onion*. (Agnus = *Ah-nyoos*)
H	Always silent. Except in two words when it sounds like *k* (a remnant from old spellings): (Hosanna = *Aw-sah-nah*) (Mihi = *Mee-kee*; Nihil = *Nee-keel*)
S	Always a sibilant sound as in *sun*, never a voiced sound as in *rise*. (Miserere = *Mee-seh-reh-reh*)
SC	Soft *sh* as in *shall* when it precedes *e, i, ae, oe*. (Descendit = *Deh-shehn-deet*)
SC	Hard *sk* as in scandal when it precedes consonants and the vowels *a, o, u*. (Scabellum = *Skah-beh-loom*)
TI	Sounds like *tsee* as in *tsee-tsee* (fly) when preceded by any letter except *s, t,* or *x* and when followed by any vowel. (Gratias = *Grah-tsee-ahs*)
TI	Sounds like a regular dental *t* as in *tee* when preceded by the letters *s, t, x* and when followed by any vowel. (Hostias = *Aw-stee-ahs*)

X   Sounds like *gs* as in *eggs* when it is at the
                beginning of a word or when it is pre-
                ceded by an *e* and followed by any vowel.
                (Exaudi = *Ehg-zaw-oo-dee*)

X   Sounds like *cks* as in *pox* in all other cases.
                (Pax = *Pahcks*)

EX   Sounds like *eck* as in *heck* when it is fol-
                lowed by a soft *c* (a *c* that is followed by *e,
                i, ae, oe*)
                (Excelsis = *Eck-shehl-sees*)

Chapter Four

Intonation Problems and Solutions

Have you ever heard yourself say, "People, you are out of tune!"? Is that helpful? First, you haven't given them any information that they can actually use. You've probably made them mad and/or hurt their feelings. All they know is that you don't like the way they sound. They do not know what is wrong with the sound, or how to change it. They really do want to get it right, but they need your help. Be the enabler here—not part of the problem.

If the intonation is suffering, try to be specific. Tell the choir if the sound is flat or sharp. If it is out of tune, it has to be one or the other. Also, address the correct section! If you are not sure, don't just guess. Have them sing it again and check it with the keyboard. When being critical of another's voice, guessing is dangerous. They would rather have you admit that you are not quite sure than have you guess wrong. It is their psyche with which you are playing.

When you determine who is out of tune and whether the sound is sharp or flat, try to determine the reason for the problem. If the reason is discovered, the solution will be forthcoming. There are many situations that can lead to out-of-tune singing. Each has a probable explanation and a possible solution.

What Causes Out-of-Tune Singing?
Singers tend to be *flat* when:
- Singing a descending passage
- Repeating more than three notes in a row
- Singing repeated passages
- Approaching the end of a long phrase
- They are vocally and/or mentally fatigued
- The rehearsal space is not conducive to good singing

Singers tend to be *sharp* when:
- Singing an ascending passage
- Singing in the stratosphere
- They are hyper

Singers tend to sing either *sharp* or *flat* when:
- Notes are insecure
- Rhythm is insecure
- Vowels are not unified
- Tessitura is difficult
- Vocal production is problematic
- Vibrato is not unified
- Trying to sing too softly
- Trying to sing too loudly

Ways to Correct Out-of-Tune Singing

1. Flat Tendencies. When singing a **descending passage**, singers will often sing the intervals carelessly—usually too wide. Knowing where the half and whole steps are is very important. Look for these troublesome phrases in the music ahead of time and be ready with the intervallic solution. This will provide you with an opportunity to reinforce the importance of the half step. It is an acoustical fact that descending half steps must be sung smaller than ascending half steps. And don't miss the opportunity to remind them to keep the "space in their face" high as that phrase descends. Singers tend to let everything collapse, especially when singing a long descending phrase. Just the opposite is true. Think high as the notes go low.

When singing a succession of at least **three repeated notes**, you can almost guarantee that the third one, and certainly what comes after it, will be low. You must sensitize them to this tendency and ask them to think that each note is actually higher than the one before it. Once this has happened several times, they can almost monitor it themselves.

The same is true for **repeated passages**. The third repetition will probably be low. Many repeated passages create boredom, hence a lack of concentration. Basses usually get stuck with these repetitive gems and have to be cajoled into believing that their part is the most important one. If they sag, the beautiful melody the sopranos are spinning above them just will not work.

Approaching the **end of a long phrase** while maintaining the pitch is such a common problem, especially among amateur and beginning singers. Efficiency of the breath is what it is all about and is one of the last skills with which they will become consistent. They run out of breath before they get to the end of a phrase and don't take advantage of the catch breath soon enough, if at all. Planning ahead for quick breaths is critical in the quest for maintaining enough breath support to maintain the pitch. Don't allow them to run out of breath. If they do, the phrase will sag in pitch. I'll look to my sopranos as they are "dying on the vine" and say, "Ladies, you ran out of breath, didn't you?" "Yes, Dr. Willetts." Again, it is a question of you sensitizing them to the tendencies. Never get that empty. Sneak a breath—reenergize and go on. Practicing the catch breath would be a good idea. We often tell choirs to sneak or stagger the breath, but how many of us actually explain that skill, let alone devise an exercise for it? Here's one that works: Repeatedly sing a short phrase and sing it continuously. Ask them as a choir to maintain a continuous sound. As individuals, they will need to catch a quick breath, but tell them not to let you catch them at it. Sneak out and back in by reducing the volume slightly, sip quickly and quietly and, yes, breathe in the middle of a word. I know, I know, you have been taught never to breathe in the middle of a word. The trick is to do this individually, not collectively; also if they breathe at the end of a word that ends with a consonant, that consonant will not line up with the other singers. If a particular phrase is beyond their breath capacity, help them identify individual spots to catch an undetected breath and ask them to mark it in their music. Building in emergency breaths is a good idea, even for the solo singer. When one is nervous, one will need more breaths. Be prepared.

If you are at the end of a long rehearsal, a long day, or a long week, give them a break. **Vocal and/or mental fatigue** are hard to fight through. Change the pace, change the seating arrangement, give backrubs, play a recording of the music, have a quiet moment, take a break. Once you hear and see that they can give no more, be happy with what they have given and send them on their way.

As to the physical properties of the **rehearsal space**, we seldom have any control. It is always too hot, too cold, too damp, or too dry. If it is too hot, everyone and everything suffers, except maybe those with arthritis. If it is too cold, you may be the only one who is happy. If you are in the basement of an older building, dampness may be a problem. In newer buildings, forced heat and air conditioning may dry out the room too much. These last two problems can be somewhat alleviated with dehumidifiers or humidifiers, whichever the case. Anything you can do to make your rehearsal space user friendly will be appreciated. Don't forget the aesthetic appeal as well. A cluttered room is unsettling to those with an obsession for neatness. Have you noticed how many people fit that category? If you do not, allow one of your qualified choir members to shine. They love to tidy up. It does not matter whose clutter, any clutter will do. An organized room could be a sign that an organized person is in charge. Good organization shows respect for your choir members, their time and talents. Do everything in your power to create an atmosphere in which they can excel.

2. Sharp Tendencies. If the singers are singing an **ascending passage**, the tendency will be to sharp. The upward swirl promotes sharpness just like the downward spiral promotes flatness. The solution is the same as for flat tendencies: to sensitize them to sing the exact intervals, especially the half steps. Going up, the intervals need to be wider, but not too wide, and the phrase still needs to be rooted in the breath. Another opposite in singing: As the phrase goes higher, think lower for the breath support. Stay well grounded in the breath.

When singers (usually sopranos in this case) are **singing in the stratosphere** above the staff, sometimes the tone becomes disconnected from the core of the breath and the pitch rises, much like a helium balloon. Let go of the string and up, up, and away goes the balloon. Keep the breath rooted and well grounded so that the intonation does not suffer.

Sometimes singers, especially children, get so **hyper** that it is impossible to keep the pitch from rising. All you can do at this point is hope that somehow they all rise together! Controlling the collective passion of a choir is something conductors need to address. You want them to be excited and into the message of the text, but if the heart overrides the brain, musical troubles could surface. It is definitely an acquired skill to balance the emotion with the mind and is usually the last thing a conductor thinks about. Don't overlook its benefits and its pitfalls. Sensitize yourself to their emotional involvement. As to a specific suggestion, remind them to stay focused and aurally centered in the key. Sometimes giving them something definite to think about and/or listen for will be just the focus that is needed to rein in the energy—energy that, if unchecked, could lead to disaster.

3. Sharp and/or Flat Tendencies. Sometimes we **mistake pitch problems for actual note problems**. They may not be singing out of tune. They may actually be singing wrong notes or insecure notes. Good for you that you hear a problem. The first step is hearing that something is wrong. The next step is to identify the real problem, then fix it. Secure the pitches and the intonation has a fighting chance.

Pitch problems can also be caused by **insecure rhythms.** If the singers know the pitches but are tentative about exactly where to sing them, that lack of security will definitely affect the pitch. A similar solution applies. Secure the rhythms and on you go.

We know that if the **vowels are not unified**, they will not tune (In chapter 2 this is discussed in depth.).

Singing in an **uncomfortable tessitura**, particularly a high tessitura, can cause pitch problems. The strain of maintaining a high pitch area for a significant amount of time is very difficult, even for a trained singer. The solution must be a vocal one that encourages "space in the face" with good breath support. Do not over rehearse these sections! If it is apparent that a section is vocally demanding, rehearse accordingly. Protect those voices. Healthy singing will bring its own reward.

Faulty vocal production can also be problematic for tuning.

This happens frequently with the male changing voices and with females who have sung only pop or country music in a chesty register. Getting everyone to sing in the correct register is no easy feat, especially if they have any significant history of singing in a forced manner. Here's a novel concept. Everyone should be assigned to the vocal part in which he or she most comfortably fits, not where he or she is most needed. Right? Who of us is guiltless? Try your very best to honor the true voice when assigning parts, knowing full well that you will have some sopranos singing alto and some baritones singing tenor. It is not fun for a baritone to always be singing practically in his falsetto voice or straining in his high register because you do not have enough tenors. If this is the case, at least let him sing baritone occasionally. Likewise, a soprano who has been asked to beef up your alto section can probably only do so by singing in that chesty quality that you are trying to avoid. Singers who are assigned to the correct part will be the most productive and the happiest. Now shall we discuss "tenorettes" or lady tenors? NO!

Here's another fun subject—**vibrato**! Some individual singers have a problematic vibrato. Is that too strong? Vibrato is a good thing, but it has to be the correct amount, which is an individual phenomenon. When a tone is freely produced, it will oscillate around the pitch center, above and below, at a unified rate of speed and in equal amounts. The "equal amounts" is the issue. There are those with vibratos that vibrate mostly on the low side of the pitch. This tends to happen with more mature singers. There are also those who vibrate on the top side of the pitch. I've come across this characteristic only with high sopranos. Don't ask me why. It probably has something to do with rarified air. There are also those with fast or slow vibratos. There are some who have very wide vibratos and there are those with almost no vibrato. In all cases the center of the pitch is distorted, and this renders the chance for good intonation to be slim. Careful placing of these problematic voices is one solution. No violence is necessary and no bodies need be left in the wake, but you'll have to read all the way to chapter 6 ("Voicing the Choir") for legal solutions to this very sensitive matter. Just know that if the basic vibrato is not unified, the intonation will suffer.

Trying to sing too softly can create pitch problems in that sooner or later, the restriction put on the vocal apparatus to "hold back" causes that apparatus to rebel. Prolonged soft singing is very difficult. The breath pressure has to be just right and that "space in the face" has to be constant. Some conductors are laboring under the false pretense that if their choir sings softly, they won't be vocally fatigued. The opposite is true—believe it! Singing at a comfortable volume for the most part and extending the volume on both ends of the spectrum (when called for in the music) will help to maintain both vocal health and good intonation.

Trying to sing too loudly can also create pitch problems in that sooner or later, the rigorous demands put on the vocal apparatus to "put out" causes that apparatus to rebel. Prolonged loud singing is also very difficult. As with singing softly, the breath pressure and the "space in the face" have to be maintained. (Is there an echo in here?) Some conductors enjoy having their choir sing *blastissimo*. Remember, "do all things in moderation."

Have I gotten your attention about the complexities of good intonation? Hearing the problems is one thing, fixing them is another. There are solutions if you will take the time and care to look and listen for them. Your choir will appreciate it and so will your listeners.

Chapter Five

Count-Singing—How and Why

Do not skip this chapter either! Let me make everyone mad right off the bat and get it over with. Singers are notoriously sloppy about rhythm. What? No argument? Singers, in general, do not sing with crystal clear rhythms. We slip and slide into and out of the rhythms (and the pitches, for that matter). Why do we do this? Because we can! Instrumentalists, regardless of the instrument they pound, pluck, strum, finger, or blow have some physical contact with an inanimate object that produces the sound. Singers do not. We cannot finger our notes. There is no resistance from which to react, no physical object to help frame our production. Our response must be internal and cerebral. So we must think like an instrumentalist and sing the pitches and the rhythms as accurately as if we were plucking, fingering, or whatever. You have no doubt heard the phrase "the musicians and the singers." (It makes my colleagues on the voice faculty at Alabama crazy when they hear this.) I'm sure the phrase is meant to distinguish the instrumentalists from the singers, but we singers are a sensitive lot, aren't we? I often tell my singers to sing as if they were playing an instrument. And I often tell my instrumentalists to sing with their instruments. It works both ways!

So how do we stamp out this sorry reputation as it relates to our musicianship, specifically to rhythm? Easy answer! We just insist that our choirs sing rhythmically! We simply hold them accountable for when to start the note and when to stop the note. Here's the hard part. **If we plan to hold them accountable, then we have to teach them how to count!** It is a question of sensitizing them to be conscious of time—the time to begin and the time to end. It is even in the Good Book—Ecclesiastes 3:1-8. We must sensitize them to the rhythmic values of the notes so that they will value the rhythmic integrity that we demand of them. In other words, we must teach them how to count-sing!

One of the many reasons for Robert Shaw's overwhelming success in the choral field was his passion for rhythm. Those of you who were fortunate enough to have worked with him will surely agree that there is no word strong enough to adequately describe his attention to the rhythmic details. You also know how to count-sing. I do not know whether this incredible technique came directly from Mr. Shaw, but it would not surprise me if it had. At the very least, he certainly popularized it. I first experienced count-singing or singing on numbers in the early 1970s when I was a graduate student at the College-Conservatory of Music at The University of Cincinnati. My major professors there were Elmer Thomas and John Leman, both of whom were in close contact with Mr. Shaw at that time. No doubt after this book is published, someone will enlighten me as to the origin of count-singing.

The "How" of Count-Singing

To count-sing, you simply sing the appropriate number of the beat with the appropriate note. You substitute the numbers of beats per measure in place of the text. In the first example you will recognize the melody of our favorite auditioning tune, "America," or "My Country 'Tis of Thee." The meter signature is 3/4. Notice the number of the beat under the appropriate note with the subdivision of the beat designated by &. It is as simple as that.

Warning 1: When first introducing this to your choir, do it with

Rhythm Exercise 1

a familiar tune. That way, the tune is automatic, and they are free to concentrate on the numbers.

Warning 2: Count-sing something at least once during every rehearsal, always with a familiar tune, and always as if it is your very favorite thing to do.

Warning 3. When first attempting to count-sing an unfamiliar piece, be sure that it is one that is not rhythmically complex. You need to build in the choir's success *because* they will hate count-singing until they get good at it. When someone in the group asks whether they could please count-sing a particular section, you will know that they have arrived!

Rhythm Exercise 2

In the second example, you will notice that I have rhythmicized the note values to indicate where I want the singers to breathe and exactly how much time they have to do it. In those places I have omitted the appropriate number and/or its subdivision in the count-singing. (Remember that rhythmicize means "shortening the note by a specific amount to facilitate a breath.") Also notice that there are two versions of the final measure. The first of the two is configured as if you were going directly to the next verse, hence the "rhythmicization" of the third beat to allow for a breath. The second version assumes that you are at the end of the piece. In this case, it is not necessary to count all three beats. Just sustain the ONE beat until the final cutoff. A conducting tip (just can't help myself): If none of the voice parts are moving during this final dotted half note, there is no need for you to beat through the THREE pattern. Just treat it as a fermata, after which you will give the cutoff. If, however, a section or instrument is moving, as in the accompaniment, you must also keep moving. Stay in charge until the piece is over.

Rhythm Exercise 3

The third example is the first two phrases of "It Came Upon a Midnight Clear," a good example of a familiar tune in 6/8. If I'm going to conduct it in SIX, I will have them count-sing in SIX. Notice that I have already rhythmicized the example. For added attention and energy to the subdivision of each eighth note, you could sing & in between each number.

The fourth example is the same tune, but should be conducted in TWO. Notice how each large beat is now subdivided by three. When possible, conduct and count-sing in the same meter.

Rhythm Exercise 4

46

The fifth example, the first eleven measures of "Joy to the World," gives us the opportunity to subdivide by four—or by sixteenth notes. It has also been rhythmicized.

Warning: Do not count-sing with sixteenth-note subdivisions until your choir has mastered the eighth-note subdivisions. Go one step at a time and be patient—persistent, but patient.

Rhythm Exercise 5

The sixth example, the same eleven measures of "Joy to the World," is count-sung in a combination of eighth- and sixteenth-note subdivisions. This version is more efficient for faster pieces with only a few sixteenth-note patterns. It is also rhythmicized.

Rhythm Exercise 6

47

The seventh example is measures 5-10 of the *Messiah* chorus, "And He Shall Purify" (bass part only). (Have to give the men equal time.) Notice that no rhythmicization is necessary.

Rhythm Exercise 7

The "Why" of Count-Singing

1. Count-singing will greatly increase your choir's rhythmic acuity. They will actually see and hear where each note fits in—when it starts, how long it stays, and when it stops. They will begin to appreciate that there is an exact place for even the shortest note, and they will do their best to get it exactly right. It is your job to sensitize them to the importance of rhythmic integrity.

2. Count-singing definitely improves intonation. If you are having difficulty with a long note passage that is sagging in pitch, ask the choir to count-sing it with eighth- or sixteenth-note subdivisions. The bubbling of the constant energy through all this activity will help keep the pitch constant. The trick here is to make them aware of the purpose of the technique and encourage them to transfer that bubbling energy as they return to the more sustained notes and text. Ask them to maintain the same energy just as they had when they were singing more actively with the numbers. Go back and forth a few times between the text and the numbers. Eventually they will believe you.

3. When the choir gets comfortable with count-singing, their

sight-reading will be greatly enhanced. There seems to be a wonderful correlation between the constancy of the rhythm when count-singing and the ability to get more correct pitches into those rhythmic slots. It's as if the rhythm is a given, which allows them the freedom to direct most of their attention to the pitches. If you only needed one reason to try count-singing, this one should do the trick!

4. The legato line is also greatly enhanced by count-singing. The constancy of an energized sound naturally connects everything until a breath is indicated. Sensitize the choir to the feeling of the constant tumbling forward action and then encourage them to strive for the same feeling as they return to the text. You may have to ask them to sing the numbers as smoothly as possible. Sometimes they will count-sing in a rough manner, especially at first.

5. The choir will be able to learn difficult passages more quickly by count-singing them first. Isolate the problematic rhythms, secure them, isolate the problematic pitches, secure them, and finally put the pieces back together. Have two sections count-sing while two sections sing text. Reverse the assignment and repeat the process. Have three sections sing text while one section count-sings. If you give each section a chance to count-sing, everyone will have sung the difficult passage at least four times. Finally, have everyone sing text, but think numbers. Drilling is not a bad thing; unless, of course, you are in a dentist's chair. (Sorry, my feeble attempt at amusing myself has no cap.)

6. Melismatic passages such as the one in Rhythm Exercise 7 are difficult to learn. Usually they are to be sung on one syllable and require considerable dexterity. If the singers have something active to sing on each sixteenth note, it is a great help. Interchange singing with numbers and singing the required syllable until they can do both well. Anything you can do to heighten the confidence of melismatic singing by amateur singers will bring its own reward.

7. Count-singing is an incredibly helpful tool for achieving great diction. You can say, "Put the *t* in the word *night* on beat 3," and they know exactly where you mean. If you really get courageous, you could say, "Put the *t* on the & of 3." It is a coveted luxury to have a choir that is highly sensitized about rhythmic integrity. Your efforts toward this end could be rewarded by hearty applause from Robert Shaw himself, though I heard once that angels make no sudden or prolonged noises.

Chapter Six

Voicing Your Choir

What does voicing your choir mean? It simply means put-ting similar voices in each section together. It is an attempt to achieve an internal blend within each section of the choir, which will then improve the overall blend that is such a vital concept in choral singing. It is a procedure to help you identify similar voices—similar in volume and vibrato. If you have a very small voice in between two huge voices, that small voice might as well not sing. There is no way that person will feel as though he or she is making a contribution. You will remember that we have already discussed vibrato in chapter 4, and I seriously doubt if we have to discuss what a "problematic" vibrato will do to the overall blend of our choirs. Blend each section first, and you will have a better chance of blending the entire choir.

How to Voice Your Choir
1. Gather one section of the choir into an area where they and you can move around. Usually the front of the room will do. Whether or not you have the rest of the choir listen is up to you. I like to have them listen because it makes them more conscious of the many vocal characteristics that make up the choir and how each can complement the other. They will even offer their opinions as to who should stand next to whom. Not that their vote matters, but they do begin to feel some owner-ship in the process and that is quite special. If you have too many people who will be too embarrassed to sing in front of the whole choir, even in pairs, then at the end of a rehearsal ask one section to remain and voice them in the privacy of their own section. If you have four sections in your choir, obvi-ously this procedure will take four rehearsals. You might try voicing the sopranos and altos in the same session and the tenors and basses at another. Sometimes you'll get better coop-

eration if they are subjected to this procedure only in the presence of their own gender.

2. Have the entire section sing the melody of at least the first few phrases of "America" *a cappella*. Use an appropriate key for each section, usually the keys of D, E, or F for the basses and altos and F, G, or A for the tenors and sopranos, and ask them to sing a comfortable *mezzo forte*. If they sing too softly it will defeat the purpose. Caution: Do not do this at the beginning of the rehearsal. They will not be warmed up vocally, and you won't get a true sound.

3. Have them sing two at a time and listen to determine if the voices blend. Is one considerably louder than the other? Is one wobbly and the other straight? Is one shrill and the other more mellow? Ask them what they hear. Ask whether they enjoy what they hear, or whether they feel as if they have to compete to be heard. Do you have some individuals in your choir by whom no one wants to sit? It may be a personality problem, but it may be a vocal problem. People will tend to sit by a voice that complements their own, even if they have not conceptualized it. If you discover two who "ping" with the same vibration, they will notice it as soon as you do. Serendipity!

4. After you have been through the section two at a time, you should be able to identify the biggest voice and the smallest voice. Ask them to stand at opposite ends of the row. Everyone else will fit somewhere in between. Assign the number 1 to the smallest or lightest voice, then have the next few small voices sing with each other to determine who will be numbers 2, 3, and 4. Always have the next voice sing with the person on either side, first one, then the other, then all three together. Some duos or trios will be immediately in sync and it will be obvious to everyone. Some will not work and that too will be obvious. Most singers will end up in the middle and could fit in several places. There is no right or wrong in finding the perfect fit. It is your personal opinion and that cannot be wrong. It may be very strange, but not wrong! Our most important responsibility is to be sure that the person whose voice does not match that particular slot does not feel inferior. It is hoped that there will be a better slot for that voice somewhere down the line. If this is a volunteer choir—most definitely!

5. Once you have mixed and matched your way all the way down to the biggest voice, start at the top again and have the number 1 voice start the theme song again. Ask each successive voice to join in, one by one, until the whole line is singing. You will need to point to each to enter. The sound will obviously get louder but should also get richer and bigger or darker. Just for fun, start at the dark end and reverse the process. Notice how the sound lightens or brightens up. Notice also that I'm using descriptive words that have no exact meaning. Only you can define your own concept of lighter or darker, thinner or richer, in sickness and in health.

6. Now you have to decide how to best use this line-up. Let's say that you have just voiced the sopranos. Your soprano section of twelve traditionally sits on the left side of the choir in three rows—three in the front row, four in the middle row, and five in the back row. Generally, the lighter voices will work best in the front row. Logic should tell us that, if the bigger voices are in the front row, that is all you will hear. The lighter voices might as well not sing. If the bigger voices are in the back row, they can go ahead and sing out. If there is an excessive amount of vibrato back there, it will have become absorbed by the time it gets to the front. The lighter voices will now feel as though they too are making a valuable contribution, and everybody is happy! And, generally, the lightest voice should be on the outside. Your line up could look like this:

Back row:　　8 9 10 11 12
Middle row:　　4 5 6 7
Front row:　　　1 2 3

Or, in a spiral arrangement:

Back row:　　8 9 10 11 12
Middle row:　　7 6 5 4
Front row:　　　1 2 3

Guess what? It does not matter. There are no rules, just your own personal taste! Experiment and see which sound you like better. Have the ladies stand in both of these configurations and let them wail away on the theme song. Listen first to determine if there is a significant difference. If there is, which one do you like? It is all up to you. If you have another section listening to this procedure, allow them to chirp in with an opinion. Everyone can get in on the act! But remember, it is still your show. Stay focused and in control.

Other Voicing Concerns

This routine does not allow for consideration of music reading ability. What happens if the three strongest readers in your soprano section turn out to be numbers 10, 11, and 12? No doubt you will want to spread them around to help any non-readers you may have. No situation is going to be perfect, so you will have to decide what is best for your choir. Compromise to find the best place for each singer so that at least your major priorities are accomplished. One of your silent priorities may be getting "Hazel" out of the front row—even though she has owned that seat for more than several years! All in the name of progress, if not peace and harmony.

This routine does help you to quickly develop a rational seating chart. You do have a seating chart, don't you? People like to know where to sit. They respond well to a routine. It also makes life easier for the attendance taker. You do have an attendance taker, don't you? Or at least you have a method by which to record attendance. The type or level of the choir doesn't matter—if folks know their absence will be noticed and notated, they somehow are a bit more reliable.

Finally, if you have a church choir and one-fifth of the choir takes a sabbatical every fifth Sunday—always a different fifth each Sunday—then this whole idea of voicing your choir is for naught. Think about this. If you have attendance problems and they are unavoidable, you work around them or you do without some key voices. You have figured this out already. Some folks just need a nudge. Perhaps if number 10 knows that she fills a spot that functions as a real link to numbers 9 and 11, and that her voice really matters in the overall blend of the whole choir, she will make choir a serious commitment. People like to be needed. And we all need new ideas on how to increase regular attendance!

Chapter Seven

Seating Formations

Has your choir been sitting in the same formation since the beginning of time? Do you sing every composition from the same formation? If your answer was "no" to both questions, skip to chapter 8. If your answer was "yes," live dangerously and read on.

As to the first question, is that permanent seating formation the best possible setup for your particular assortment of singers? Does it enhance their overall performance? As to the second question, have you considered temporarily moving for the sake of specific types of music? Moving your singers into different locations can give a whole new meaning to the phrase "being in the right place at the right time."

In this chapter you will find many mixed-choir seating possibilities with rationales for each. They are divided into two categories, the first for choirs in the *ideal* category—those having well-balanced sections; and the second, for the *real* world—those with unbalanced sections. An ideally balanced choir is a personal choice in that it is what you personally want to hear. My personal ideal, give or take a few, would be equal numbers of basses and altos, one or two more sopranos, and one or two fewer tenors. Good tenor voices seem to have more ringing power and can override a bass section if given half a chance. All this, of course, is determined by the individual strength of the voices. You may have a few super altos and not need as many. On the other hand, you may have mostly lightweight sopranos and need more. No two situations are alike and one person's ideal may be another's trash. One or two of the following treasures may be useful and adaptable to your unique situation.

Note: In seating formations that involve an eight-part division, the upper case letters signify the higher part (S = soprano I), and the lower case letters signify the lower part (s = soprano II). In basic four-part setups, only upper case letters are used.

Well-Balanced Sections

1. This basic setup is probably the example most universally used. It works well when combining with instruments in that the high to low voicing from left to right matches the voicing of the string quartet, the woodwind quintet, and some variations of the brass quartet or quintet. It also promotes efficient cueing, especially in much of the Baroque and Classical music, in which the instruments often double the voices. Also, the listener has equal access to all the parts. Many large symphonic choirs are seated in this formation. It works well with the standard seating of an orchestra.

Ex. 7.1

S S S A A A T T T B B B
S S S A A A T T T B B B
S S S A A A T T T B B B

2. The opposite of Example 7.1 is probably the next most popular example. This setup seems to be the most logical for two reasons: (1) most conductors are right-handed, which often relegates most of the gesturing to the right hand; and (2) the melody lies mostly in the soprano part. However, when instruments are added, the cueing becomes very problematic, as does the overall sound.

Ex. 7.2

B B B T T T A A A S S S
B B B T T T A A A S S S
B B B T T T A A A S S S

3. Another version finds the women on the outside. This maintains equal access for the listener and promotes better tuning by putting the outside voices together. The disadvantages here are that when the women sing in a duet fashion, the ensemble may suffer somewhat, and, when using instruments, the appropriate doublings may not align properly.

Ex. 7.3

```
SSSBBBTTTAAA
SSSBBBTTTAAA
SSSBBBTTTAAA
```

4. Keeping the women on the outside, but reversing the men has no redeeming features, unless of course, it is your personal favorite.

Ex. 7.4

```
SSSTTTBBBAAA
SSSTTTBBBAAA
SSSTTTBBBAAA
```

5. In a well-balanced situation, the opposite of Example 7.3, putting the men on the outside, has no merit either; but "leaving no stone unturned," it would look like this:

Ex. 7.5

```
BBBSSSAAATTT
BBBSSSAAATTT
BBBSSSAAATTT
```

6. The expanded version (eight-part) of Example 7.1 maintains equal access for the listener, as well as compatible high to low voicing to best match the orchestra. Remember that the upper case letters signify the first part and the lower case letters, the second part.

Ex. 7.6

```
SSssAAaaTTttBBbb
SSssAAaaTTttBBbb
SSssAAaaTTttBBbb
```

7. Notice in this version that the voices that tend to dominate (soprano I, alto II, tenor I, and bass II) are in the back, and those voices that tend to need some enhancement (soprano II, alto I, tenor II, and bass I) are in the front. The

sections are still identifiable, and the bigger voices are out of the front row. Everyone is happy.

Ex. 7.7

S S S S a a a a T T T T b b b b
s s s s A A A A t t t t B B B B

8. The next several examples do not offer equal access to the listener from left to right, or right to left, but do offer more of a two-dimensional, stacked type of sound with two sections in the front and two in the back. In general, men's voices tend to be louder than women's voices. By putting them behind the women, the overall sound is much more homogenized. Notice how the soprano and bass voices are still in close proximity to promote good intonation.

Ex. 7.8

B B B B T T T T
B B B B T T T T
S S S S A A A A
S S S S A A A A

9. Examples 9-11 are variations of Example 7.8, the difference accounting only for taste. Example 7.9 shows the basses and tenors reversed.

Ex. 7.9

T T T T B B B B
T T T T B B B B
S S S S A A A A
S S S S A A A A

10. Here, the altos and sopranos are reversed.

Ex. 7.10

T T T T B B B B
T T T T B B B B
A A A A S S S S
A A A A S S S S

11. This grouping is the same as Example 7.8, except that the sopranos and altos are reversed.

Ex. 7.11

B B B B T T T T
B B B B T T T T
A A A A S S S S
A A A A S S S S

12. The eight-part version of Example 7.8, my personal favorite, looks like this. Notice again that the dominant voices in each section are behind their respective counterparts.

Ex. 7.12

b b b b T T T T
B B B B t t t t
S S S S a a a a
s s s s A A A A

13. This example allows for a more equal distribution (left to right) of sound among the women and the men respectively.

Ex. 7.13

B B b b T T t t
B B b b T T t t
S S s s A A a a
S S s s A A a a

14. This arrangement was a favorite of the late Paul Christiansen. It uses a principle quite similar to orchestral seating in that the first chair of each section is the best musician in the section and becomes the section leader. Number 2 is the next best, and so on. I'll extend this chart to demonstrate how it would look if we had a choir of forty with five on each part. The section leaders, or number 1's, are on the inside and the numbers work outward. Notice with this setup that you could immediately identify a solo octet by simply asking all the number 1's to sing. They are all right there in the center.

Ex. 7.14

```
b  b  bb  b  t t t  t t
B B B B B T T T T T
s  s s s s  a a a a a
S S S S S A A A A A
(5 4 3  2 1  1  2  3  4  5)
```

15. Here is a four-part formation for which you must have not only equally strong voices throughout the section, but each section must be equally strong as well. If you have the voices, this does sound wonderful. The listener hears all the parts coming forward at the same time. It produces a layering effect that is all-inclusive.

Ex. 7.15

```
B B B B B B B B
T T T  T  T T T T
A A A A A A A A
S  SS  S  S  SS  S
```

16. Extend Example 7.15 into an eight-part group and have an instant double choir formation just by separating them down the middle. All the firsts are in Choir I (on the left), and the seconds are in Choir II (on the right).

Ex. 7.16

```
B B B B      b b b b
T T T T      t  t t  t
A A A A      a a a a
S  SS  S     s  s  s  s
```

17. Another dual-purpose version, this formation produces a wonderful stereophonic sound when singing just SATB and offers the required double choir effect when necessary.

Ex. 7.17

```
S S A A T T B B   b b t t a a s s
S S A A T T B B   b b t t a a s s
S S A A T T B B   b b t t a a s s
```

18. And for the fanciest of this version, put the seconds of each section in the center and surround them on both sides with the firsts, thereby leaving the lower (or heavier) voices in the middle and working your way out in both directions to the higher (or lighter) ends. This produces a rich sound that seems to have no division.

Ex. 7.18

```
B B b b b b B B
T T t t t t T T
A A a a a a A A
S S s s s s S S
```

19. Many choirs enjoy the luxury of singing in mixed quartets. I say luxury because this assumes that you have singers who are independent enough to carry their own part regardless of what they are hearing from their nearest neighbor. The immediate advantage from singing in mixed quartets, aside from the social value, is the tuning. If a few singers stray from the center of the pitch, they are less likely to disturb the whole section when standing in this formation. They hear how their note fits in with the whole chord and not just the same note in the whole section. They will also be more alert for a longer period of time! Notice that both Examples 7.19 and 7.20 preserve some definition for the listener in that there are similar streams of sound coming forward.

Ex. 7.19

```
S A T B S A T B S A T B
S A T B S A T B S A T B
S A T B S A T B S A T B
```

20. Move the basses next to the sopranos for a variation of Example 7.19 and you will preserve that similar stream as well as facilitate a gender mix.

Ex. 7.20

S B A T S B A T S B A T
S B A T S B A T S B A T
S B A T S B A T S B A T

21. For the ultimate in the true scrambled effect, reverse the direction of the middle row and obliterate the similar streams. This is choral singing at its most participatory best! You can still control the balance of the overall sound by assigning the larger voices to the back rows.

Ex. 7.21

S B A T S B A T S B A T
T A B S T A B A T S B A
S B A T S B A T S B A T

22. Try a totally random scatter just for fun. (The word *random* infers that they individually choose where to sit as opposed to being amicably subjected to where you want them to sit—a choice you *must* make when diving into these fresh waters.) Ask them to move beside a person who sings a different part. Total chaos will reign initially. Just give them a minute and they will find a spot. The more social creatures will love this, but some of the more delicate souls might be embarrassed. Keep a sharp lookout and perhaps suggest a place where you know they will be comfortable. You'll be amazed at some of the pairings that pop up. The end of a rehearsal is a good time to do this. Introduce it as a reward for their hard work.

Ex. 7.22

B S T A T S B A S A T B
A B T S B T A S T S B A
T S B A S B T A B T A S

23. If singing from a mixed formation interests you, but not all of your singers are that independent, consider using a modified mix. Creatively seating the dependent singers can allow you the luxuries of a mixed formation without demoralizing

anyone and without losing the contribution of any of your singers. This version also retains the streams of similar sound.

Ex. 7.23

```
S S B B A A T T S S B B A A T T
S S B B A A T T S S B B A A T T
S S B B A A T T S S B B A A T T
```

24. Here we can preserve the security of two on a part but negate the similar sound stream.

Ex. 7.24

```
S S B B A A T T S S B B A A T T
T T A A B B S S T T A A B B S S
S S B B A A T T S S B B A A T T
```

25. Another version of a modified mix is to internally mix each half of the choir.

Ex. 7.25

```
S B S B S B A T A T A T
S B S B S B A T A T A T
S B S B S B A T A T A T
```

26. To avoid the similar sound streams mix each half of the choir and reverse the middle row of each half.

Ex. 7.26

```
S B S B S B A T A T A T
B S B S B S T A T A T A
S B S B S B A T A T A T
```

Unbalanced Sections

And now to the real world! Most of us, at one time or another, have had to produce music on a regular basis with an irregular number of singers. The most common problem is not enough tenors and more than enough sopranos.

27. If your weakest section is really weak, put them front and center and wrap them in strength.

Ex. 7.27

SSSSBBBBAAAA
SSSSTTAAAA

28. This version keeps the tenors well positioned without separating the soprano from the alto sound.

Ex. 7.28

SSSSBBBBSSSS
AAAATTAAAA

29. If you want to partially preserve the high-to-low sound flow, this version might be useful.

Ex. 7.29

SSSSAAAABBBB
SSSSAAAATT

30. If your women greatly outnumber your men, keep the few you have happy and surround them with kindness.

Ex. 7.30

SSSSSSAAAAAA
SSSSBBBAAAA
SSSSTTAAAA

31. If you have the reverse situation, the men outnumbering the women, I want to hear about it!

Ex. 7.31

BBBBBTTTTT
BBSSSAAATT

32. Often in church music, the physical properties of the chancel dictate our seating formations. If the organ console is

centered and faces the choir, you may have fewer rows in the center. Actually, this is not a bad situation. The wrap-around effect enables the singers to hear one another even though the spatial distance may be significant.

Ex. 7.32

```
S S S B B B B A A A
S S S T T T T A A A
S S S        A A A
```

The Performance Space

Speaking of the "wraparond effect," allow me a word in general about the performance space. **If your particular space permits, curve your choir into a semicircle by pulling the ends of all rows toward you,** making sure that each row remains intact and the curved lines are even on both sides. This will enable them to hear one another better, thus improving the possibility of better ensemble and better intonation. If your semicircle gets very deep, you will have to ask the singers on the ends of the rows to turn slightly (on an angle) to the front, rather than face directly across to the opposite side. If they are facing directly across, the listeners will hear mainly the singers in the center since they are the only ones facing directly forward. You will hear everyone because you are right there. You are surrounded by the sound. This is a great way to rehearse, but in the performance situation it will rob the listeners of a well-balanced sound. Get someone to listen for you, or better yet, go out into the performance area and listen for yourself. You will be amazed at how different they sound from a distance. Try to put yourself in the listeners' place when you are making decisions that may be affected by acoustical properties. It adds yet another dimension with which you must be familiar.

If your physical space permits, have the singers spread out with room for another person between each singer. Sound will seek its own space. If you have twenty singers crammed together, usually for the sake of musical security and/or tradition, they will have a certain sound. If you spread them out, the sound will be greatly enhanced both in terms of tone and volume. This is an acoustical phenomenon, not my imagination. Crowd the space and you crowd the overtones, therein confusing the overtones. (This is one reason why instrumentalists get really annoyed when they don't have their own personal acre of land from which to play.) If you simply don't have the space, at least use the entire space that you do have. Crowd the singers and you stifle the sound. Space them out and you free the sound to seek its own space and its true timbre.

Whatever the configuration of the performance site, try to rehearse in that same configuration in the rehearsal space. I have witnessed many disasters when the choir always rehearses in a particular seating arrangement and then suddenly moves to a different arrangement for the performance. Singers, particularly amateur singers, get used to the sounds around them, and it provides a comfort level that contributes to their sense of security. This should not be taken lightly. Disturb that comfort zone, and you may have an insecure singer.

Without much discussion, we can all agree that at least one rehearsal in the actual performance space is a critical advantage, and that rehearsing the arrival and departure of the choir is a critical necessity. It can be annoying to an audience when the choir's movement is sloppy or confused as they enter and exit the performance area. Make sure your choir not only sounds good, but looks good as well.

Moving Sections to Enhance Specific Styles

Now that you have determined the ideal seating formation for your choir, I'm going to risk asking you to change it again. **Consider that not all music is best served by the same seating formation.** For this discussion we will focus on three types of compositional styles:
1. Polyphonic (fugal and/or imitative)
2. Homophonic (unison rhythm among all parts) with diatonic harmonies
3. Homophonic with dissonant harmonies, tone clusters, or atonality

A fourth variety would be those pieces that have elements of more than one type of compositional style. Certainly, polyphonic pieces have homophonic sections just as basically homophonic pieces have some imitative sections. You will have to decide what the majority of the piece will need in terms of enhancement by alternative seating. Each individual piece will have its own set of determinants. **1. Polyphonic/fugal.** The individual lines of the fugue subject and the countersubject, or themes, should be heard. If the choir is seated in sections, the listener has a good chance of hearing the lines individually. From the Well-Balanced Sections seating formations, Examples 7.1 through 7.7 would be ideal. Examples 7.8 through 7.14 would work in that the sections are intact, but the listener does not have equal access to all of the sections since only two are represented in the front row. Examples 7.15 and 7.16 further muddy the waters because of the sections being stacked—even though the sections are intact. None of the mixed or modified mix formations are appropriate in that none of the sections are intact. Such formations could diffuse the fugal subjects to the point of total chaos. Example 7.17 might effect an interesting phenomenon in that the listener would hear three of the fugal subjects stereophonically.

Sometime when you have rehearsal time left over, try a fugal piece from several different seating formations and let a few of the singers listen from afar. They and you will be amazed at the difference of the sound, all caused by a different seating formation. If they buy into the concept that one seating formation may not be appropriate for every piece, they will be much more mobile in thought and deed!

From the Unbalanced Sections category, Example 7.29 would probably work best, although 7.27, 7.30, and 7.32 would certainly be acceptable. Example 7.28 would create a stereophonic effect with the women.

2. Homophonic with diatonic harmonies. With homophonic pieces with basically diatonic harmonies, we are free to investigate the many possibilities that can enhance the overall sound, not to mention better blend and better intonation, all without worrying about individual lines becoming blurred.

From the Well-Balanced Sections, certainly Examples 7.1 through 7.18 would not be wrong, but Examples 7.19 through

7.22 would be ideal. Example 7.21 would be my personal choice. It provides a total mix of both genders and sections and also provides the listeners with the most homogenized sound possible, as well as the most fun for the singers.

From the Unbalanced Sections, Example 7.28 offers the best situation for enhancement of tone and intonation. Actually, you could use a modified mix among the women (we'll number this one 7.33) if they are musically strong, but probably, because of their small numbers, you will need to keep the men together.

Ex. 7.33

    S A S A B B B B S A S A
    A S A S A T T S A S A S

3. Homophonic with dissonant harmonies, tone clusters, or atonal sections. If your choir is musically strong throughout all sections—the ideal of the Well-balanced Sections—you could afford to choose Example 7.21, even for most of the really difficult music. Professional choirs, church choirs that are predominantly paid choristers, or advanced university choirs that consist of mainly graduate students with a few upperclassmen would be able to handle a challenge of this magnitude. For most of us, we'll go directly to the modified mix possibilities. Any of Examples 7.23 through 7.26 would be possible. However, if "safety first" is your motto, go back to Examples 7.7 through 7.18 and concentrate on getting the notes and rhythms correct.

4. The Unbalanced Sections category—forget it! You are not going to program music of this description anyway. Stick to what your group can do well and celebrate their enthusiasm and faithfulness.

Now that you have decided to play this adult version of musical chairs, a word of caution is necessary. In a situation where several different seating formations are used in the same service or concert, rehearse getting into and out of those positions thoroughly. You must prepare this movement as a choreographer or a general readying his (her) troops for battle. If you have natural gifts for this sort of task—great! You will be in your element. If your visionary resources are coming up blurry, assign this task to one of your eager beavers who has shown some interest and/or creativity in moving furniture with efficiency. To move the choir members in between pieces does take a great deal of thought and practice. Be sure that this thought and practice are on your or your assistant's part and not on the part of your choir. Do not take up their rehearsal time to figure all this out. You will get far too much help from everyone, and no one will be happy! You make the decisions ahead of time and then execute them with confidence. It would not be a bad idea to write out the instructions so that you will not be tempted to make adjustments at the last minute. If they sense that you are making it up as you go along, your punishment will be death by stabbing—perhaps with your own baton! Well, have we exhausted this subject, or what? I'm sure that I have missed a few seating possibilities, and I'm equally sure that I will hear about them. You can be sure that I will pass them on—in the *next* millennium.

Chapter Eight
Score Study and Score Preparation

The word *preparation* has been used in this document numerous times, but nowhere is it more appropriate than here.

You have just chosen a piece for your choir to sing and you feel confident that you have made a good choice. I just happen to have a copy for us to look at together.

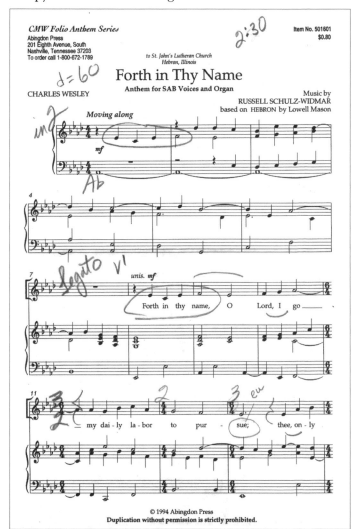

"Forth in Thy Name" by Russell Schultz-Widmar (Abingdon Press, #501601)

The next step is to prepare it for the first rehearsal. You must examine it from every angle, and you must be completely comfortable with it before that first rehearsal. Do not expect to learn it as your choir does. Even if you are a "quick study," the preparation you do in advance will help identify possible trouble spots so that you can think ahead about possible solutions. Also, the time it takes you to learn it should give you a clue as to how long it will take them to learn it.

Here are four areas of preparation for your thorough enjoyment: (1) score analysis; (2) musical preparation; (3) textual preparation; (4) and conducting preparation.

Score Analysis

As we look at the first page, notice that the piece was written for St. John's Lutheran Church in Illinois. Check out the city and check out the name of the hymn tune. Clever! If you don't point this out, the retired English teacher in the second row may delight in exposing your neglect at finding such a delectable tidbit. And who is Lowell Mason? He just happens to be one of our most important early music educators. If you are a Methodist, you know who Charles Wesley is. If you're not, look him up. Mr. Schultz-Widmar is an unknown to me, but one phone call to the publisher should help because there are usually fact sheets on all of the company's composers. Huzzah! They did! You will discover that Mr. Schultz-Widmar was born in Illinois in 1944 and is now with the Episcopal Theological Seminary in Austin, Texas, and the Episcopal Church of the Good Shepherd in Austin.

Now you are ready to analyze the piece from a structural reference point. This is not just an exercise. You will see that your discoveries will guide your decision making all along the way. This is the place to start.

Let me offer a few words about the graph on the next page, even though it is relatively self-explanatory. The measure numbers read from the biggest sections to the smallest possible sections. Verse 1 is eleven measures altogether, but it can be broken down into 6 + 5. We can break down the first of the two phrases even further into 3 + 3. When you are trying to arrive at the

Structural Analysis Graph   "Forth in Thy Name" Schultz-Widmar
Basic form: strophic, four verses

Intro	Verse 1		Verse 2
Measures 1—7,	8——————18,		19—————29,
	8———13, 13———18,		19—24, 24———29,
	8-10, 11-13, 13———18,		19—22, 22—24, 24—26, 27—29,
Phrases: 7, +	3 + 3 +	5,	3 + 3 + 2 + 3,

Organ	Choir (unison)	Canon at the octave (not strict)
Head motif		Men/women
1st four notes		diminution in women's part
in treble clef		for cadential purposes

A-flat major ————————————————————————————

Interlude	Verse 3		Interlude	Verse 4
30——33,	34—————44,		45—46,	47——————57
	34———39, 39—44,			47—52, 52—54, 55—57
Phrases				
4, +	5 + 6,	+	2, +	5 + 3 + 3

Organ	Choir (*a cappella*)	Organ	Choir
	Three-part harmony	head motif	men & altos, melody
	melody in soprano	same music	soprano descant
	(exact)	as 1-3	

A-flat major————————————————————————————

number of measures in each phrase, don't feel that you have to be exact. You will have many partial measures. Look at measure 13, for example. One phrase ends and another begins. It is not necessary to work with partial measures. There is such a thing as too much detail! Make your best decision and move on. I chose to count measure 13 as the end of the phrase because the last three notes in that measure function as a pickup to the next phrase. That next phrase feels as though it begins in measure 14. The point of this analysis is to help you decide where to phrase, or where to breathe. When you actually prepare your score for conducting, this information will be put to good use.

I would also be proud to mention the teacher from whom I learned this valuable routine, Julius Herford. He actually called this graph a "structural memorization graph." In 1967, as a master's student at Indiana University, I was too young to realize that I was in the presence of such a great mind and such an incredible influence in the world of choral music. All I knew was that he was German and scared me to death. Many of my young students today do not even know the name Julius Herford. Leonard Bernstein and Robert Shaw both knew and respected him. If they had a question about anything connected with the great choral masterpieces, they would call Dr. Herford. In fact, that was how I first met Robert Shaw. He had come to Bloomington for a weekend of study with Dr. Herford, and Mrs. Herford insisted that his students come to their home for a light repast and heavy observing. We were thrilled and grateful. I'm still grateful and will do my part to keep his name in the forefront of choral music. If you want to delve deeper into this area of study, see *Choral Conducting Symposium,* edited by Harold Decker and Julius Herford.[8]

Musical Preparation

1. Play through the accompaniment (no matter how slowly) to get the piece "in your ear." Notice in measures 10-13 that the accompaniment is higher than the melody. This might cause a problem initially. Also notice that in measure 18 the head motif appears again in the accompaniment. It sets up the canon of verse 2 nicely. Verse 3 is *a cappella* so a cue to the organist at measure 44 would be appreciated (assuming you are not on the bench yourself).

2. Sight-sing (*without the piano*) each vocal part. If you miss a note or a rhythm, chances are your choir will too. With this forecast you can have your solution ready.

3. Next, sing one part and play the one next to it. Follow this routine until you have worked your way through all the parts.

4. Now play two parts in every combination possible. It helps to see and hear how the parts interact. Internal octaves or unisons will be helpful to lock in for tuning purposes. Identify these, then circle them in your score. Encourage your choir to

do the same. It will help sensitize them to listen to what happens around them.

5. After all this getting acquainted, if there are still problematic rhythms or pitches, devise some appropriate drills. They may come in handy later.

Textual Preparation

Since I have already decided on a *legato* articulation, I want the text to be linked as much as possible. Remember the rule: If new words are formed, don't link! If you must link some text, don't link so aggressively.

I have marked my score at places where I know I will have to offer verbal instructions. Marking them provides clues that help me to prioritize my listening.

1. Measure 13—the *Daniel Sitteth* rule
2. Measure 14—*rih*, not *ree*
3. Measures 21 & 22—open *ah*, the first sound of the diphthong, sustained
4. Measures 22 & 23—no *R* in "cheerful"
5. Measures 25 & 26—another long beat diphthong
6. Measure 26—*eh*, not *uh* in presence
7. Measures 38-39—for the musical line, "substance" linked with "see" (Use one *S*. Otherwise it is too awkward.)
8. Measure 42—no *R* in "offer"
9. Measure 47—no *R* in "For"; "*dih*-light"
10. Measure 53—*th* of "with" pronounced as a sibilant
11. Measure 55—*th* of "with" and the *th* of "thee"—voiced and combined for one smooth sound

Conducting Preparation

1. Choose your tempo, meter, and basic articulation and mark your score! Mr. Schultz-Widmar has given us only a small clue about the tempo, and though he has metered it in quarter notes, I choose to conduct this in half notes. My version is going to move along with less vertical beating from me. I also want a very *legato* sound, and beating it in TWO rather than FOUR will promote that. Though the meter is often a good clue as to how to conduct the piece, it is not a given. Experiment to see what

works best for the music. If it is different, don't be hesitant to change it. Notice that I have changed all the 6/4 measures to 3/2. Clearly, the musical and textual accents fall every other quarter note, not every third.

2. Now to rhythmicizing—if there is a comma that I do not want to observe, I will put a slur across the comma (see measure 9). If I want a breath and have to make room for it, I'll put in the appropriate rest (see measure 11). These internal phrases correspond with the structural analysis that has already been done. Notice that I have not phrased all the verses alike. Look at measure 22. Why would I need to rhythmicize the top line? Remember that I'm beating half notes. It will be easier to rein-force the cutoff of the sound of *nd* if I'm on a full beat. More important, having the women clear the A-flat before the men sing G will be an improvement. As to measure 26, phrasing both parts together is preferable to my ear. In measure 29, the same reasoning was applied as in measure 22. This is just a personal choice, not a rule. The few places where I have inserted eighth rests may provide encouragement to my singers to get a quick breath so as to re-energize for the next phrase. They will have a tendency to take too long for the breath and be late for the next entrance.

3. Other marks you will see on the score are arrows for cue-ing, vertical circles to quickly alert me to listen for unisons and/or octaves, and horizontal circles beginning in the first measure in the accompaniment that identify notes that function as a head motif for the tune.

4. Do not neglect physically practicing the actual conducting of this piece! There are no great technical difficulties other than the changing meters and giving good preps at the beginning of phrases that begin on a partial beat, as in measure 8. At first glance the meter changes seem to be the same for each verse. Au contraire! A closer examination reveals that in verses 1 and 4 the meter changes fall between the same number of measures, but in verses 2 and 3, specifically at measures 25 and 40, there is only one 2/2 measure between the 3/2 measures. In verses 1 and 4 there are two measures at those places. This difference may seem insignificant; but, if it helps your conducting, it is very significant indeed. Thinking and acting like a well-prepared conductor will sensitize you to detail in a hurry.

Imagine your level of confidence when you walk into that first rehearsal with all of this preparation behind you! The best part is that your confidence will be contagious. It will spread throughout your choir and there will be no limit to the heights you can reach together.

Chapter Nine

Rehearsal Planning

Every bit of planning you do for a rehearsal is an act of self-defense, in that this planning allows you to make the most of your own rehearsal time. It also allows you to enjoy the fact that you know you can get from point A to point Z in a given time frame. Knowing this allows you to be confident, and confidence allows you to perform at your highest level. That's the long way around to encourage you to plan ahead!

Below you will find three rehearsal planning routines, all of which will help you to see the proverbial "light at the end of the tunnel." We are going to assume that you have programmed Vivaldi's *Gloria* and have eight weeks to prepare it. You have one rehearsal per week, each lasting ninety minutes. (Do not include your dress rehearsal as one of the eight. Schedule it as an extra event.) In this ninety-minute rehearsal, plan for seventy-five minutes of actual rehearsal. Announcements, warm-ups, and general housekeeping chores will absorb fifteen minutes. The first routine will map out a rehearsal schedule for this eight-week period; the second will map out one sample rehearsal; and the third will deal with the dress rehearsal, which includes the orchestra.

The Long-Range Rehearsal Plan

Even though this routine is centered around Vivaldi's *Gloria,* it can be adjusted to fit any kind of concert or service. The *Gloria* has nine choral movements. If your program has individual pieces, just use them in place of the individual movements. You can also adapt the routine to a church choir situation in which you have a "performance" every week. Most church choir directors work six to eight weeks ahead. You will just have one or two pieces rotating off each week as you add one or two to be sung six to eight weeks later. *(Have I lost you already?)* The specifics are not as important as the concept.

Make it fit whatever circumstance is necessary. Also know that you will have to make adjustments along the way. I have yet to stick to a long-range rehearsal plan exactly! If I have planned to rehearse four movements at a particular rehearsal and only get to three, then obviously an adjustment needs to be made. The best time to assess the situation is immediately after each rehearsal. If your rehearsals are at night, you're usually wired and cannot shut down immediately anyway. If possible, before leaving the premises, check off the "done" items on your individual rehearsal plan and reschedule the "left undone" items. While the rehearsal is fresh in your mind, make notes on the priorities for the items you did rehearse when their turns come up again. Now, don't you feel smug with your next rehearsal all planned, and it isn't until next week?

The first step in developing the master plan is to make several charts, the first of which is a chart of all of the movements (or pieces). Include vocal forces, tempo, number of measures, duration, and instrumental forces. Duration is a critical piece of information, but it can be determined only after you have decided what your tempos are going to be. Don't just list them from the back of a CD. Invest in a stopwatch or at least a watch with a second hand big enough to see and trust your own musical judgment.

Vivaldi's *Gloria*

CHART 1 | **TWELVE MOVEMENTS**

1. Gloria in Excelsis	2. Et in Terra Pax	3. Laudamus Te
Chorus	Chorus	Duet (S & S)
Allegro	*Andante*	*Allegro*
72 measures	92 measures	125 measures
2:15	5:00	2:15
Tutti orch.*	Strgs+cont.**	Strgs+cont.

4. Gratias Agimus . . .	5. Propter Magnam . . .	6. Domine Deus
Chorus	Chorus	Soprano
Adagio	*Allegro*	*Largo*
6 measures	19 measures	43 measures
:30	1:00	3:30
Strgs+cont.	Strgs+cont.	Oboe+cont.

7. Domini Fili . . .	8. Domine Deus . . .	9. Qui Tollis
Chorus	Alto+Chorus	Chorus
Allegro	*Adagio*	*Adagio*
98 measures	40 measures (24 chorus)	20 measures
2:15	4:00 (2:00 chorus)	1:00
Strgs+cont.	Strgs+cont.	Strgs+cont.

10. Qui Sedes . . .	11. Quoniam . . .	12. Cum Sancto . . .
Alto	Chorus	Chorus
Allegro	*Allegro*	*Allegro*
150 measures	23 measures	78 measures
2:30	:45	3:00
Strgs+cont.	Tutti orch.	Tutti orch.

* *Tutti orch.* = All the instruments play. In this case "all" will include oboe, trumpet, violin I, violin II, viola, cello, bass, and keyboard.
** *Strgs+cont.* = Abbreviations for strings and continuo. *Continuo* refers to the bass instruments plus the keyboard; i.e., cello, bass, and harpsichord or organ.

CHART 2   **CHORUSES BY TEMPO**

Allegro	*Andante*	*Adagio*
1. (easiest)	2. (longest)	4. (only 6 measures)
5. (only 19 measures)		8. (with alto; only 24 measures for Chorus)
7. (very rhythmic)		
11. (same music as no.1)		9. (only 20 measures)
12. (hardest—double fugue)		

CHART 3   **SOLOISTS**

Soprano	Alto
3. Duet	3. Duet (assuming she can match the soprano)
6. Aria with oboe	8. Aria with Chorus
	10. Aria

CHART 4   **INSTRUMENTS**

Strings & Continuo	Oboe	Trumpet in C
1. through 12	1, 6, 11, 12	1, 11, 12
(violins & viola tacet on 6.)		
(*Tacet* means "to be silent")		

Now the fun begins! Add up the timings of the choruses:

2:15	5:00	:30	1:00	
2:15	2:00	1:00	:45	
3:00				
7:30	7:00	1:30	1:45	=17:45

Round the grand total to eighteen minutes of music that the chorus must learn. Remember that we are working with seventy-five minutes of our rehearsal, and we have eight rehearsals. That computes to six hundred minutes. We have approximately eighteen minutes of music to learn and approximately six hundred minutes in which to do it. Sounds like a lot. I feel better already!

If my rehearsal plan was to simply run through all the music each rehearsal, in order, and without really rehearsing, I would just run all of the nine choral movements four times each (18 x 4 = 72). I'd have three minutes left over! Not a good plan. People enjoy the process of working out the details. If you allow them to sing wrong notes or rhythms too many times, they become frustrated. They do want to get it right!

My favorite rehearsal plan is to rehearse each movement five times within the course of the eight rehearsals:

1. Introduce and read through.
2. Read again and begin to work.
3. Work hard.
4. Begin to polish.
5. Finish the polishing.

My next step is to work with the timings of the movements and determine how long I can rehearse each piece. I'm going to spare you the grief of trying to mathematically work this out by using all nine movements. With some of them being so short, it was an exercise in futility! So, back to the drawing board, or in this case, Chart 1. Notice that movement 4 is only :30 and it segues right into movement 5. Notice also that movement 8 segues into movement 9. Let's investigate rehearsing all four of these short movements as one unit for a combined total of 4:30. Add movement 11 (:45) to movement 1 (2:15) for a total of 3:00. They are basically the same music anyway. Now we have a more equitable and workable time distribution.

Movements 1 & 11	=	3:00
Movement 2	=	5:00
Movements 4, 5 & 8, 9	=	4:30
Movement 7	=	2:15
Movement 12	=	3:00

Do this using measures as well:

Movements 1 & 11	72 + 23	=	95 measures
Movement 2			92 measures
Movements 4, 5 & 8, 9	6+19+24+20	=	69 measures
Movement 7			98 measures
Movement 12			78 measures

With this revised information, let's agree to work with these five units rather than with nine movements. Now we are getting somewhere! Five units rehearsed five times each equals twenty-five rehearsal slots. Let's say I want to rehearse each unit twenty-five minutes (25:00) each. It would look like this:

$$5 \times 5 = 25 \times 25 = 625$$

Close enough! Actually, to make it come out almost perfectly, I'll rehearse four units for twenty minutes (20:00) each at the first rehearsal (take five minutes less warm-up time) and then three units for twenty-five minutes (25:00) each at the remaining seven rehearsals. Remember that I have seventy-five minutes (75:00) per rehearsal and eight rehearsals. All is well. Now it looks like this:

75:00 x 7 rehearsals	=	525 minutes
20:00 x 4 units	=	80 minutes
		605 minutes

Actually, that extra five minutes comes out of our warm-up time. It is not tacked onto our allotted ninety-minute rehearsal. So, perfection has been achieved, at least on paper.

The next challenge is to block in the specific units on the appropriate rehearsals. List the units again, and, if possible, put your calendar on the same page. As you block in your units, check beside them so that you can keep track of how many times you've used them. After all this work, you do not want to leave anything to chance. Include a general tempo so that you can be sensitive to tempo variation as you make your decisions.

Chart 5   Rehearsal Calendar

<u>Units to rehearse</u>

1 & 11	fast	/////
2	slow	/////
4, 5 & 8, 9	s-f-s-s	/////
7	fast	/////
12	fast	/////

<u>Week 1</u>
1 fast
2 slow
7 fast
4 s-f-s-s

<u>Week 2</u>
1 fast
4 s-f-s-s
12 fast

<u>Week 3</u>
2 slow
7 fast
12 fast

<u>Week 4</u>
1 fast
2 slow
4 s-f-s-s

<u>Week 5</u>
4 s-f-s-s
7 fast
12 fast

<u>Week 6</u>
1 fast
2 slow
12 fast

<u>Week 7</u>
1 fast
4 s-f-s-s
7 fast

<u>Week 8</u>
7 fast
2 slow
12 fast

<u>Dress Rehearsal</u>   <u>Performance</u>

Notice that not more than one week goes by without any unit being rehearsed. The worst thing to do is to learn one movement completely before going on to the next. By the time you get to the last movement, either you may be out of rehearsal time, or when you return to the first movement at the dress rehearsal, the choir may have forgotten it. Bring all of the movements along together. Also notice that by the end of the second rehearsal, they will have seen all the music at least once. That in itself is comforting. If you have misjudged how difficult a particular section may be, you have plenty of time to adjust.

Speaking of time, you must make a valiant effort to honor both the starting and stopping times, as well as the internal twenty-five-minute (25:00) intervals within each rehearsal. If you spend this much time on a plan, you should certainly follow it! Besides, if you can build a reputation for being timely, it makes a strong statement as to your respect for their time as well as your organizational capabilities. Two more reasons for saint-hood!

The Individual Rehearsal Plan

Earlier in this dicussion I listed a five-stage rehearsal plan. Let me expand upon those concepts before we build our individual plan.

1. Introduce and read through. As you introduce a piece to your choir, the best thing to do is to let them sing it once through (all the way through) without interruption. I usually say to my choir, "If the accompanist and I are the only ones actively participating, we will stop. Otherwise, hang on. If you get lost, listen around you and try to get back in." For the good readers this will be the highlight of their evening. It is downhill from there as they wait patiently for everyone else to learn the notes! Reward them and challenge the others. You will also be rewarded by how the slower readers rise to the challenge. If this becomes a routine, they will begin to expect it and actually count on it. They and you will enjoy monitoring their progress at sight-reading. If the piece is relatively short, I will simply have them read it again. It is amazing how many things get fixed without our interference.

2. Read again and begin to work. The second time this piece comes up in the rotation, read it again and then begin to "stop and fix." I try to let three mistakes go by before I stop. Early on, I would be so energized to actually hear the mistake, I would gleefully stop after hearing only one! "A-ha! That's a B-flat, tenors, not a B-natural!" What I failed to realize is that all this stopping and starting de-energized the choir. It is truly a drag to stop so often. The choir never gets a sense of the entire section, not to mention the individual phrase. Let them sing! Find a way to memorize the mistakes as they go by and then fix at least three at a time. One might be a note problem; one, a rhythmic problem; and one, a text problem. Fix the glaring problems first. Think of the music as a chunk of clay and you as the potter. (Does this remind you of a hymn?) You chip away a little at a time and eventually you have a beautiful pot, or in this case, a piece of music. When your allotted time for this piece is up, be willing to go on to the next piece and leave the current one in its imperfect state, confident in knowing that there will be another day!

3. Work hard. This is your main work rehearsal. In preparation for it, you will have identified the spots that still need technical attention. Go directly to those spots. Do not waste time by luxuriating through the music that already sounds good. Fix the little things, then go back and reinforce the nearest connections. If time allows, go back and run the entire section or movement. You also need to begin to listen for balance and nuance and to be more demanding of dynamics and style.

4. Begin to polish. At the fourth rotation, run the movement while still listening for all the aforementioned items. Isn't it amazing how spots that you thought were fixed are broken again? You can never stop listening. You have to fix it again. Ask whether it was an individual or whether the whole section needs help. Usually, if it was one half-asleep person, he or she will confess and you can just go on.

The priority is to get the music "off the page." That is to say, create music! Guide and encourage them to sing with such verve and such spontaneity that even the most lethargic listener will take notice. These are the fun rehearsals when the music is almost ready. You sense it and, if you convey that, they will sense it. The pot is about to be unveiled, and everyone is on task to make it happen. The music is about to come "off the page" and into the expectant ears of the audience/congregation/ passersby/ whomever! The Tuscaloosa Symphony Orchestra performs in the wonderful Moody Concert Hall in the School of Music on some Monday evenings. Unfortunately, the Tuscaloosa Community Singers rehearse on Monday evenings. When the two events coincide, I cannot resist a momentary and sudden shift in my rehearsal plan when the symphony audience is enjoying their intermission. We shift immediately into whatever music is at the stage of "off the page," and the passers-by are royally entertained. If they like what they hear, they may come to our concert as well.

5. *Finish the polishing.* If things have gone according to Hoyle and not Murphy, this last rehearsal should be a confidence builder. If some things are still a bit shaky, at least you have this time to get it all together.

A word about calling extra rehearsals—DON'T! If you cannot get the music ready in the allotted time, the fault is yours. Don't add to the choir's time to fix your problems. You chose the music, and you set up the schedule. You either overestimated the ability of your group, your initial planning was ambitious, or your rehearsal technique is less than adequate. Is this too strong? I know, there are always extenuating circumstances. I can hear it now, "But my people are absent too much. If they are not there, how can I do my thing?" Sorry, part of "your thing" is to see that they are there! That's part of the responsibility of the conductor. You might have lost a whole rehearsal due to a snowstorm (in Alabama?) or some other unforeseen event. Most of your people will be willing to adjust. Respect their time, and they will be more willing to give it.

In the individual rehearsal plan (Chart 6), I've chosen Week #5 from Chart 5. Notice that we have listed movements 4, 7, and 12 to be rehearsed. First, reorder the movements to take advantage of the tempo variations. Rehearse movement 7 first, then movement 4, and finally movement 12 (*fast, s-f-s-s,* and *fast*). It will be the third rehearsal for both 7 and 12, so they will be in the "work hard" stage. For movement 4 (remember to include 5, 8, and 9), it will be the fourth rehearsal, putting you at the polishing stage.

Directly related to the Vivaldi, movement 4 begins with chorus and orchestra performing at the same time. There is no instrumental introduction from which the choir can get a pitch. When this happens, remember to rehearse getting from the preceding movement to the beginning of the next movement. Don't even think about giving the choir pitches between the movements! Movement 4 also segues into movement 5. The same situation occurs between 8 and 9. Be sure to practice getting from one movement to the next for that initial pitch security. Wasn't it fortuitous that we decided to rehearse these movements as a single unit from the start?

Chart 6   An Individual Rehearsal Plan
<u>Week 5</u>
Warm-ups   Physical   7:30
                Breathing
                Vocal Exercises (from chap. 2—nos. 1, 3, & 4)
                Change no. 4 to dotted rhythms to set up the
                first piece to be rehearsed, movement 7.
                Reinforce separating for the dot.

7. *Domine Fili* (third rehearsal – "work hard" stage)   7:45
Check men: Measures 53-70 for pitch and rhythmic
        security.
Check tenors: Measures 28-37—then all sing.
Check alto line: Measures 79-84—then all sing.
Run from top. Reinforce dotted rhythms and separating
        for the dot.

4. *(4, 5 & 8, 9)* (fourth rehearsal – "begin to polish" stage) 8:10
8. *Domine Deus*
Add soloist, start measure 11.
        Insist on more decay on weak syllables.
Ex. Peh-KAH-tah, disappear on *tah.*
Check togetherness of "s" in measure 28.
        In measure 35, a slight separation of each syllable
        in *miserere;* should be a pleading sound.

9. *Qui Tollis*   8:20
Segue from movement 8 to cement initial pitches.
Encourage sopranos to sing with courage in measure 16.
Run twice.

4. Gratias Agimus / 5. Propter Magnam　　　　　　　8:25

　　Segue from end of movement 3 (ends in G major,
　　　　G now becomes the third of E minor).
　　In the opening word, *Gratias,* work to get through
　　　　the consonants *Gr* and to the vowel *ah* at the same
　　　　time.
　　Segue to movement 5.
　Continue to encourage a detached articulation on first
　　　four notes of the theme.
　Work for uniformity of vocal production on melismatic
　　　passages.
　Continue to resist their tendency to ritard into final
　　　cadence.

12. Cum Sancto Spiritu (third rehearsal – "work hard" stage)
　　　　　　　　　　　　　　　　　　　　　　　8:35

　　Secure beginning pitches in measures 23-25.
　　Then run section.
　　Secure beginning pitches in measures 50-51.
　　Run section.
　　Rehearse altos, tenors and basses in measures 73-75 for
　　　　ensemble of rhythm and text.
　　Start back at measure 55 and run to end.
　　Run from top.

If time allows, run the movement again and ask them to stand when they are singing the first theme. Otherwise, sit but continue to sing. (This is a double fugue, and this exercise is in the name of *educational fun*). Entice them with a parting thought that next week they will have the opportunity to stand when they are singing the second theme!

AMEN　　　　　　　　　　　　　　　　　　　　9:00

The Dress Rehearsal with Orchestra

　Refer to Charts 3 and 4. These show which movements the soloists sing and which movements the instrumentalists play, respectively. Organizing your orchestra rehearsal is very critical. It makes a strong statement to everyone involved that you are a professional and can be trusted with matches. (Strike that!) Being capable of thinking of more than one thing at a time is also noted—consideration of their time as well as the music.

You can approach this rehearsal with at least three different priorities, depending on who will benefit the most: (1) the choirs' level of comfort with the new accompaniment; (2) the soloists; or (3) the instrumentalists. A fourth priority could be the music itself. A fifth priority cannot be for your benefit! As usual, you have to do all your rehearsing privately.

Several factors will help you to determine which of those priorities will be the most desirable for your particular situation. It is possible to combine several of the above and keep almost everyone happy.

First, are your players volunteers or will you be hiring them? If hiring, will it be a union gig or are your players professional but not unionized? If you are hiring, do you have enough resources to hire them for two rehearsals and the performance? This would mean a total of three services. (Chapter 10 deals with the care and feeding of your local troubadours.) Let's assume that you are going to hire a combination of students and faculty from the local area, but you have only enough money for one ninety-minute rehearsal and the performance.

You have enough money to hire a small group of strings, but your oboe and trumpet players are volunteers. The local high school band director is a fine trumpeter and a member of your congregation, and his wife plays the oboe. Hey! It could happen. You have one ninety-minute rehearsal, and the whole piece takes approximately thirty minutes. What are your organizational choices?

The easiest thing to do is to just start, fix as you go, and hope that you will get to the last movement before the bell rings. You must stop, of course, at the appointed time, even if your entire group is made up of volunteers—especially if they are volunteers! They will be that much more willing to play for you the next time. If it is a hired group, they may very well get up and leave, even if you are not through. They will hold you to the contracted time, and they have every right to do so.

Musicians have fought long and hard for good working conditions. Don't you fight against it.

The next easiest choice is to just run the entire piece once, go back and fix glaring problems, and if time allows, run it again. For both of these options, everyone sits "at the ready" the whole time. This is not a thoughtful use of anyone's time.

The least easy option (least easy for you, but the most efficient one for everyone else) will take careful planning on your part. What a surprise! However, you will be the benefactor as this will translate into a more efficient use of everyone's time.

You start at 7:30 P.M. That means a downbeat at 7:30 sharp! Here are two plans. Version 1 requires everyone to be there at the beginning but allows the trumpet and oboe an internal break. After playing their movements once, they must return for the run-through for the last thirty minutes. Version 2 allows the trumpet, oboe, and soprano to arrive later by grouping their performance times together. Also, this version gives the alto a rest before the run-through.

Chart 7		**Two Dress Rehearsal Plans**	
Version 1		Version 2	
1	Tutti*	7	Choir & Orch.
11	Tutti*	2	Choir & Orch.
12	Tutti*	8	Alto, Choir, & Orch.
	(Trpt. break)	9	Choir & Orch.
6	Sop., Oboe, & Cont.	10	Alto & Orch.
	(Oboe break)	3	Sop., Alto, & Orch.
3	Sop. & Orch.	4	Choir & Orch.
	(Sop. break)		
4	Choir & Orch.	5	Choir & Orch.
5	Choir & Orch.	6	Sop., Oboe, & Cont.
2	Choir & Orch.	1	Tutti*
7	Choir & Orch.	11	Tutti*
8	Alto, Choir, & Orch.	12	Tutti*
9	Choir & Orch.	Run in order.	
10	Alto & Orch.		
Run in order.			
*excluding soloists			

Though both of these plans would work, I chose Version 2 to work out the actual timings. I have sixty minutes to play with since I will need the last thirty minutes for the run-through. To arrive at these all-important times, I refer again to Chart 1 to get the running time of each movement. I double the actual time and round up to the nearest whole number and use the remaining few minutes as insurance.

Chart 8   **The Final Rehearsal Plan**

7.	Domine Fili	Choir & Orch.	(2:15)	5:00	7:30
2.	Et in Terra Pax	Choir & Orch.	(5:00)	10:00	7:35
8.	Domine Deus	Alto, Choir, & Orch.	(4:00)	8:00	7:45
9.	Qui Tollis	Choir & Orch.	(1:00)	2:00	7:53
10.	Qui Sedes	Alto & Orch.	(2:30)	5:00	7:55
3.	Laudamus Te	Sop., Alto, & Orch.	(2:15)	5:00	8:00
4/5.	Gratias/Propter	Choir & Orch.	(1:30)	3:00	8:05
6.	Domine Deus	Sop., Oboe, & Cont.	(3:30)	7:00	8:08
			(1:00 catch-up)		8:15
1.	Gloria	Tutti*	(2:15)	5:00	8:16
11.	Quoniam	Tutti*	(:45)	2:00	8:21
12.	Cum Sancto	Tutti*	(3:00)	6:00	8:23
		(1:00 to reassemble for run-through)			8:29
Run-through		30:00		30:00	8:30

  *excluding soloists

AMEN   9:00

Make copies of this schedule, put a copy on each music stand, and give one to each of the soloists and choir members. Their immediate reaction will be one of shock and disbelief. Don't be insulted. They'll get used to it. Make Chart 8 large enough to see and have a large-faced watch or clock nearby or on your music stand. You don't want to waste precious time trying to focus on your wristwatch. You would do well to practice this routine as part of your own private preparation.

After spending as much time with this piece as it will take you to develop these plans, think how comfortable you will be with it. Confidence, my friends! Confidence!

Chapter Ten

Instrumental Accompaniment

Choral conductors who want to conduct their own performances of major works rarely have as much podium time as their instrumental counterparts. The resident orchestra is usually contracted for three to five rehearsals, and depending on the length and complexity of the work, one or two include the chorus. That means the instrumental conductor, whether he (rarely she) is the resident conductor or a guest conductor, will have two rehearsals with the orchestra alone, then two more with the chorus and the orchestra. He will also have come to the chorus for a piano rehearsal before the orchestral rehearsals start. If the choral conductor hires a pickup group, generally there is only enough money to hire them for one rehearsal, and it is seldom enough time to run through the piece more than once. Yet, we are criticized for all kinds of inadequacies in handling an orchestra. We have one-fourth to one-fifth the amount of podium time as the orchestral conductor. Fair or not, we are held to the same standards. Pardon another cliché, but, "if you can't stand the heat, don't play in the kitchen." If choral conductors want the opportunity to conduct the works that require large instrumental forces, they need to devote a great amount of time preparing themselves completely! Most of that preparation is done, as we have stated before, in private, and without a practice instrument. Our only chance for a successful experience is our own preparation, and that preparation includes carefully organizing our one and only rehearsal. OK, let me get off my soapbox!

Adding instrumental accompaniment to your choral offerings can be challenging; but it can be very rewarding as well, not only for you but also for your singers. Inexperienced choral conductors are often very nervous about jumping into these waters, not knowing how deep they can be. For some it is really a leap of faith. Tighten your life preserver and leap away. With diligent preparation and compassionate instrumentalists, it can be an exhilarating experience.

First, this chapter will not be the definitive source for your instrumental edification, but will provide helpful hints for survival in the trenches. Let me recommend two wonderful books that deal much more completely with this subject: *The Modern Conductor* by Elizabeth Green, and *Face to Face with an Orchestra* by Don Moses, Robert Demaree, Jr., and Allen Ohmes. [9]

Second, please allow me a personal moment (again!). In an ideal world, you would always use the prescribed instrumentation when planning for your instrumental accompaniment. In a practical world, however, you might be tempted to use whatever your resources will allow. Here is the argument: "I want to do the Berlioz *Requiem,* but I don't have enough money to hire an orchestra large enough. I'll just use the organ." On the one hand, your choir may never get to experience this piece unless you do it with a simplified accompaniment. On the other hand, will their experience be a worthwhile one since this version will be extremely depleted of its colorful instrumentation and the very essence of Hector Berlioz? I can hear the furor now! I cannot answer this question for you. I merely want to present the problem—and then run—hoping, of course, that you will struggle mightily with your own decision making.

While you struggle, think about the true motivation behind your choice of repertoire. Is the Berlioz *Requiem* the right piece for your group? Will it showcase them at their best, or is your personal desire to perform the piece the overwhelming motivational factor? And the answer is . . . I'm still running!

The instrumentation prescribed in the full score will determine what instruments you are going to use; but in regard to the strings, it will not tell you how many of each to use. If the piece calls for violins I and II, viola, cello and bass, and your choral group is small to medium (sixteen to thirty-two singers), the least you can get by with is a string quartet. It is preferable to have the lower octave that the bass provides, but if resources are low, you could do without this instrument, especially if the keyboard is going to be organ. By thoughtfully registering the pedal stops, you can get that octave here. Usually the left hand (or pedal) of the organ, the cello, and the bass all play the same bass notes. If you do use a quartet, be sure that your players can handle what in essence is a solo part, and share this information with them from the start. If they walk into the one and only rehearsal and discover they are the only one on the part, it could cause a mild trauma, particularly if they are not aggressive players.

If your choir is larger and you have the resources to hire a respectable string section, try to hire at least three on a part. Less than three (except for one) becomes a tuning problem. It seems that three players will meld into one pitch, but two will struggle. That third opinion is like an arbitrator. A simple majority wins. The combination of 5, 4, 3, 2, 1 (that is, five first violins, four second violins, three violas, two celli, and one bass) will do nicely. Now I know I just said use at least three on a part, but I have suggested only two celli. Having the bass as part of the bass complement will give you that third player, albeit an octave lower, to homogenize the pitch. Remember that the bass and cello most often play the same music. In fact, they generally play from the same part. If the cello is to play alone, it will be so designated in the score. Also, three celli would not be a good balance for three violas. The higher the instrument is pitched, the more players you will need.

You have determined your instrumentation and you are ready to secure your players. *To secure* would imply that you have put together a budget and know approximately how much you have to spend. There is no dollar amount I can give you. The figures below are merely examples. What the going rate is in one area may be totally out of line in another, and there could be as many as five different pay scales. If it is a union gig (all the players belong to the musicians union), only union members can play and everyone gets paid according to scale–the union scale, that is. A local person will need to put you in contact with the local union representative so that you can function with some sense of security. The categories below represent a combination of player resources, and the rate would be per service. (A service is a rehearsal and/or a performance. If you have two rehearsals and one performance, that would be three services. The rate is the same for both occasions.)

- The majority of players will get $50.
- The first chairs of each section will get $60.
- The concertmaster could get $100 if he assists with the bowing.
- Students or less-experienced players may get $30.
- Volunteers will get the largest thank-you notes.

Find a busy instrumentalist who will advise you as to the going rates and then try to match your resources to your musical goals.

Perhaps this checklist will be of assistance as you go from the first decision about your instrumentation up to the performance time.

1. **Major decisions to be made:**
   a. Choose repertoire and performance date or dates.
   b. Determine how many rehearsals you will need, the number of players you will need, and how much you can pay each one. Arrive at the "bottom line" figure. How much is it going to cost?
   c. Determine the source or sources of the necessary funds or start over and choose less expensive repertoire. Assuming the best, we'll move on.

2. **Contract your players yesterday!** You cannot do this too early, especially if your concert is during a peak concert season like Christmas or Easter. If you wait until a month before your event, the best players will be booked solid. Six months, even a year in advance is not too early.

3. **If you have a trusted instrumental captain or contractor, let that person contract the group for you.** However, you will have to pay for this luxury. Often this person will be one of the players you hire, and usually you will pay him double his playing salary. Tell him the amount you can pay per service; the number of services there will be; and, of course, the dates and times. Also, give him a deadline to have all the players confirmed. This keeps everyone on the same page.

4. If you contract the players yourself, you can save the fee of the contractor, but be prepared to get very comfortable with the telephone. Start a phone list of players and keep it updated. It will come in handy the next time.
5. Create a very simple contract with a tear-off bottom. This provides you and the players with a paper trail that is beneficial to all parties. They keep the top half with all of the particulars and return the bottom half with their signature to you. An example follows:

Name: _____

Instrument: _____

Repertoire: _____

Rehearsal date and time: _____

Performance date and time: _____

Fee: _____

Please return this bottom half to room 163 by September 1.

Repertoire: _____

Instrument: _____

Signature: _____

6. Order the score and the parts. Your music distributor can help you with this. Sometimes the scores are for sale, but often they are available only for rental. Get the telephone number of the publisher and ask for the rental department. Identify the name of the work you want to rent, how many of each string part you will need, the performance date or dates, the name and type of the performing group, the name of the conductor, and your mailing address. If I have missed anything, they will catch it. Be sure to tell them if you are a non-profit group, as this will be a factor in determining the cost. They will quote you a price that includes the performing rights and the rental fee. Based on standard procedure, you will receive the material one month prior to the first performance, and you must ship it back soon after the last performance. Ask for the conductor's score ASAP! They are very good about honoring that request. The other special request: "May I have clean copies" is more difficult with which to comply. It doesn't hurt to ask. These rented scores and parts are often so marked up that one can hardly see the notes. The instructions, "Mark only in pencil and erase all marks before returning the materials," are not always followed. Check the music as soon as it arrives to see first, whether it can be seen, and second, whether all the parts are there. Keep the original mailing cartons if they are reusable. As to payment, some publishers will accept a purchase order number and send you an invoice later, but others like to have the money in advance. Tell them what you are able to do, and they will work with you. Dealing with rental folks is not for the faint-hearted. They are not mean-spirited, they are just busy! If you have all your information at hand, and sound as if you have done this before, you'll have their full attention.

   7. **Study the full score and put in all your marks**—in pencil, of course. (Review chapter 8 if necessary.)

   8. **Mark the parts.** Giving the players clear roadmaps will help to keep them on course and focused on the task, and will save you much rehearsal time. Verbal instructions take time and may be forgotten by some, while others take time to write them in their parts themselves. Using your score as a guide, transfer anything that is appropriate to the individual parts. Do it yourself! It provides extra study time for you. Seeing all that music go by in each part is not time wasted. (If you have never played in an instrumental group, it also gives you a visual clue as to how little they have from which to play. It is a bit scary to play with confidence when you have only one part in front of you. That's why they need a conductor! They depend on you to paint the big picture.) Do not assign this task to an assistant unless you have a lot of strings. You mark one part for each string section and then get help copying those marks into the appropriate sections. Sometimes the first chairs will put the marks in for their sections. Large orchestras have paid librarians, part of whose job description is to mark all the parts. I know this is tedious and time-consuming, particularly if your instrumental group is large, but it saves you time in rehearsal, and time, in this case, *is* money. Just so we leave no

stone unturned, here is a checklist within a checklist for these marks, which you are so diligently going to make!

- Tempi and conducting meters
- Any subdivisions
- Phrasing to match the choir
- Reducing dynamic markings if you anticipate a balance problem
- Correcting note or rhythmic mistakes (special credit if you find them first)
- *Ritardandi* or *accelerandi*
- Tempo changes, some that may be proportional
- Possible cuts
- Highlighting special dynamics
- Little eyeglasses at spots where you would appreciate their own eyes on you
- At the end of the piece, remind them to leave the music on the music stand after the last performance. This last item is pretty much standard procedure for the players, but you may have some rookies in your group. It will save you tracking them down later and retrieving the part. Of course, you must remember to collect them from the music stands before your volunteer stage crew clears the stage. You might also check the music stands after the rehearsals as well. Some experienced players who do not need to practice in between may leave the music there, fully expecting it to be right there for the next rehearsal or performance.
- Unless you are an experienced string player, *do not bow the string parts yourself.* Ask your concertmaster, or a respected string player to do the bowings. If they are not done ahead of time, you will have to allow rehearsal time for them to be decided upon and disseminated back through the sections. It is critical that the players within each section have the identical bowings. As a conductor you should be very familiar with string terminology as it relates to sound and articulation, but do not presume to give them technical advice. When I am unclear about the sound that I want, my patient con-

certmaster asks me to sing the articulation to him, and then he translates it into "stringese." Together we arrive at the best possible sound with the appropriate string articulation. Remember that you are all on the same side—the side of the music.

9. Take note of awkward page turns. It will be to their liking and to your advantage if you have photocopied, cut, and pasted so that there is no interruption in the music. This is especially important if you have one player on a part.

10. Make a photocopy of all the parts before you distribute them. Once they are out of your sight, you do anticipate seeing them again, but one never knows. Many rehearsals and/or performances have been saved because someone was able to supply an insurance copy to replace the one the dog had for lunch. Be prepared. If these are rental copies, of course you must destroy the photocopies after the final performance.

11. Distribute the parts at least two weeks ahead of time. Not all the players will practice their part, but hope springs eternal. It usually depends on the complexity of the music and on how busy everyone is. Expect them to be sight-reading at the rehearsal. If they come prepared, it will be a pleasant surprise. When you distribute the music, include a short photocopied memo reminding them of the rehearsal and performance times. Also include information about the concert dress. This will save time by avoiding questions (and answers) in rehearsal.

12. The day of the first rehearsal has finally arrived. At least forty-five minutes ahead of time have the rehearsal site ready (yes, you need a stage crew) with chairs and stands exactly where you want them. Know who sits where. In the case of the strings, ask your contractor or your concertmaster to help you decide who will partner best on each stand. The stronger player will be on the outside. If you are unsure about how to seat an orchestra, consult either of the two books I have already recommended. Players, just like singers, are creatures of habit and will expect to sit in a standard place. If your performance site has limitations that force you to be creative with the seating arrangement, try to consider all the possible ramifications such as bowing room, volume, timbre, acoustical problems, close proximity to players in the same family of instruments, as well as sight-lines to you. As the players arrive (they will usually come early and warm up), greet them and introduce yourself. Extra special credit if you know and remember each of their names!

13. As to rehearsal breaks, an hour and a half is the longest you dare go without a break. If your rehearsal runs for two hours, at least ten minutes should be scheduled for a break. Plan these breaks so that the second part of the rehearsal is shorter. For example:

Rehearsal	1:00 P.M – 2:10 P.M.
Break	2:10 P.M – 2:20 P.M.
Rehearsal	2:20 P.M – 3:00 P.M.

If you rehearse for two and a half hours, plan a twenty-minute break. For example:

Rehearsal	1:00 P.M. – 2:20 P.M.
Break	2:20 P.M. – 2:40 P.M.
Rehearsal	2:40 P.M. – 3:30 P.M.

If it is a union gig, find out what the local rules are.

14. The day of the performance has arrived. You are still standing!

   a. Check the performance site, as it may have gotten rearranged since you last saw it.

   b. Be sure the lighting is sufficient for everyone concerned. If the players and singers cannot see, don't expect them to perform well.

   c. Put a program or bulletin on each stand.

   d. Put their checks on their stands. They will expect to be paid at the performance unless you have made other arrangements ahead of time. Put each check in the correct envelope, especially if you are not paying everyone the same amount.

15. If you are taping the event, video and/or cassette, and have secured the necessary permissions, check with your tech-

nical wizard. He or she may need to have the timings of each movement in case the tape needs to be turned. Aren't you glad you have them at the ready? (See chapter 9, chart 1, page 82.)

16. Plan your curtain call. Doing all this musical work and then forgetting to recognize someone, or doing it haphazardly, will detract from the beautiful music you have just made. Try this order:

1. Vocal soloists
2. Chorus
3. Instrumental soloists
4. Remaining instrumentalists (Shake hands with the concertmaster and get everyone up. Don't forget the keyboardist.)
5. Conductor

Notice that you are last—not first! Remember that you have not made a sound. If there is space and time to exit and return for another bow, let the soloists go first. Cue the choir ahead of time to stay in position until it is clear that you and the soloists will not be returning for that seventh bow. Again, as the conductor, you are last out, last to bow, and last off.

17. The day after, or as soon as you recover, thank-you notes would be in order. They are not necessary, but are always appreciated. If your players were volunteers, they are a must!

Conclusion

Though it has been more time-consuming than I had originally planned, I have thoroughly enjoyed writing this book. I am glad to share whatever I have absorbed over the past "umpteen" years. Here's hoping that I will continue to learn! Surely we can agree by now that the breadth of knowledge the complete conductor needs to have at his or her fingertips (no pun intended) is staggering. A conductor's preparation should be multifaceted and, admittedly, can be a lifelong pursuit. But the amount of time devoted to the study of conducting in an undergraduate curriculum at most colleges and universities is embarrassingly little. That could be one reason why so many of you spend so much time in workshops! You want and need more education.

What if you and I join together in an all-out campaign to increase the number of courses required by all prospective conductors? Can it happen? Will it take another lifetime? Let's do it. Let's hound the Boards of Education, the state agencies that govern curricular matters, the committees on committees—whoever will listen. If we are successful, we will have more young conductors who are better trained and have a better handle on the craft as they begin this lifelong endeavor. Music education in our schools and in our churches needs a boost. Who is going to do the boosting if not this next generation of conductors?

Well, this conclusion is turning out to be a possible introduction to the next book! Nay! Nay! My golf game has suffered enough. Suffice it to say, join me on the links, and we'll talk about the preparation of conductors—or not.

Notes

1. Sandra Willetts, *Upbeat Downbeat: Basic Conducting Patterns and Techniques* (Nashville: Abingdon Press, 1993), pp. 17-29.
2. *The American Heritage Dictionary* (Boston: Houghton Mifflin Company, 1992).
3. Milton Drake, Al Hoffman, and Jerry Livingston, "Mairzy Doats," copyright © 1943.
4. Ibid.
5. Madeleine Marshall, *The Singer's Manual of English Diction* (New York: G. Schirmer, 1953).
6. John Moriarty, *Diction: Italian, Latin, French, German* (New York: E. C. Schirmer, 1975).
7. *The Correct Pronunciation of Latin According to Roman Usage* (Philadelphia: St. Gregory Guild, Inc., 1937, renewed GIA Publications, 1965); John Moriarty, *Diction: Italian, Latin, French, German* (New York: E. C. Schirmer, 1975); *Translations and Annotations of Choral Repertoire, Volume I: Sacred Latin Texts*, compiled and annotated by Ron Jeffers (Corvallis, Ore.: earthsongs, 1988).
8. *Choral Conducting Symposium, 2nd ed.*, ed. Harold Decker and Julius Herford (Englewood Cliffs, N.J.: Prentice Hall, 1973, 1988). See especially chapter 5, "The Choral Conductor's Preparation of the Musical Score" by Julius Herford.
9. Elizabeth Green, *The Modern Conductor, 3rd edition* (Englewood Cliffs, N.J.: Prentice Hall, 1969, 1981; Don Moses, Robert Demaree, Jr., and Allen Ohmes, *Face to Face with an Orchestra* (Princeton, N.J.: Prestige Publications, 1987).